613 3/22

Chandler.

How to have good health.

DATE DUE

**FIRST BAPTIST CHURCH
LIBRARY
TOMBALL, TEXAS**

How to Have Good Health

1982
This Book
presented to the

CHURCH
LIBRARY
IN MEMORY OF

Mrs. Lou Stephens

BY

Dorcas Class

Code 4386-23, No. 3, Broadman Supplies, Nashville, Tenn. Printed in USA

HOW TO HAVE GOOD HEALTH

E. Ted Chandler, M.D.

BROADMAN PRESS
Nashville, Tennessee

© Copyright 1982 • Broadman Press
All rights reserved.

4252-98

ISBN: 0-8054-5298-2

Scripture quotations marked NASB are from the *New American Standard Bible*. Copyright © The Lockman Foundation, 1960, 1962, 1963, 1971, 1972, 1973, 1975. Used by permission.

Quotations marked NIV are from HOLY BIBLE *New International Version*, copyright © 1978, New York Bible Society. Used by permission.

Quotations marked Phillips are reprinted with permission of Macmillan Publishing Co., Inc., from J. B. Phillips: *The New Testament in Modern English*, Rev. Ed. © J. B. Phillips 1958, 1960, 1972.

Quotations marked RSV are from the Revised Standard Version of the Bible, copyrighted 1946, 1952, © 1971, 1973.

Quotations marked TLB are taken from *The Living Bible*. Copyright © Tyndale House Publishers, Wheaton, Illinois, 1971. Used by permission.

Dewey Decimal Classification: 613
Subject headings: HYGIENE//PHYSICAL FITNESS//CHRISTIAN LIFE
Library of Congress Catalog Card Number: 81-68045
Printed in the United States of America

Dedicated to
Fran, Lynn, Steve, David, and Krista

Preface

After completing the schooling that qualified me to practice medicine, I thought that my job as a doctor was to recognize and treat illness in my patients. I did just that, but, along the way, found that I couldn't do it without considering how that illness disrupted the lives of my patients.

The nature of illness, then, took on a different meaning. It could be as simple as a case of hives from nervousness or strep throat treated and cured with ten days of Penicillin. Those are the easier cases in medicine. But the lives of many patients were affected in a major way by illness. In particular, those with heart disease, stroke, cancer, and chronic illness were driven into discouragement and despair by the changes those illnesses wrought in their lives.

Modern technology has improved the ability of the doctor to diagnose an illness with accuracy, but, to a great degree, the skill and knowledge to reverse the effects of these chronic diseases has not yet arrived. Acknowledgment of this fact confirms the need to sustain and encourage these patients. At the same time significant advances have been made in the knowledge needed to teach prevention to those likely to become victims of these same diseases. The problem in the area of prevention has been one of faulty interpretation and failure to apply those facts we have learned.

It is the intention of this book to impress each of its readers with the wisdom of the Creator, who, through the act of creation, placed each of us individually, in balance or in equilibrium with our environment. Illness results when that balance is disrupted, but even then all is not lost. Doctors and medicines are extensions of the plan of God's creation and, as such, become the patient's allies against illness. The doctor, though, even when he is an instrument of God, doesn't always have the skill to cure illness or cannot always offer a reasonable hope of recovery. He can, however, encourage an examination of the closeness of the patient's walk with God. The patient's attention is then directed to the source of hope, peace, and promise.

The beginning of a disease may be silent, yet the basic fault in an artery or cell will grow to the point that a symptom develops. It is at this point that the meaning of the symptom is sought for and interpreted by the doctor.

Doctors have never been strong encouragers of prevention of disease, because it has not been clear which advice was the right advice. Many readers will have an avid interest in this and I believe the advice contained in these chapters to be correct. This material evolved from my study of disease prevention; undertaken because I believed that my patients needed to know and could use such facts. Much of the material has also been used to teach courses in health at my church.

I have become a better doctor from the writing of this book. My understanding of the nature of illness and patients has deepened. I more clearly recognize the thread of doubt that binds the life and strangles the spirit of the one ill. Yet, I recognize, without doubt, that the solution to that problem is the relationship of the patient to the Savior. I hope that every reader will examine that relationship in the search for health and peace of mind. The doctor shall one day be the patient and he needs that strengthening force, with its promise of everlasting life, no less than each reader or each of his patients.

Contents

1. Persons in God's World — 11
2. The Diseased Heart — 21
3. Human Nature—Worried Sick — 32
4. Cancer—A Threat to Life — 48
5. Human Nature—Seeking Healing — 58
6. An Assessment — 72
7. A Healthier Heart — 79
8. Eating to Live — 95
9. God's Nature—Healing — 121
10. The Doctor—God's Instrument — 139
11. A Blueprint for Change — 151
12. Faith—Its Role in Sickness — 171
13. Thoughts on Doctoring — 179

1
Persons in God's World

And God said, Let us make man in our image, after our likeness and let them have dominion over the fish of the sea, and over the fowl of the air, and over the cattle, and over all the earth, and over every creeping thing that creepeth upon the earth. — Genesis 1:26

In the beginning God created. . . . Genesis takes us back to the all-important moment of creation when God spoke into being the matchless wonders of sun, moon, stars, planets, galaxies, plants, moving creatures, and Adam, whom he made in his image.

The beauty, complexity, and orderliness of the human body continue to unfold as the progress of medical science illuminates the darkest corners of the function of our cells. Daily we see the evidence of God's wisdom as we watch the motion and energy of our bodies accommodate to the trials and joys of living. We are self-contained beings, seeking to find happiness in an environment which may be unreceptive and less than kind.

The unkindness of the environment begins with the journey of birth. We are propelled forward in a gush of fluid, narrowly escaping choking and barely avoiding strangling from the connecting cord that gave us life for those months of existence within the uterus, and stimulated into breath through the hands of the stranger who caught us. Passage from this beginning through the years of dependence to a state of independence, without life's threats taking their toll, is miraculous within itself. Yet, 99 percent of us are born healthy, and to reach adulthood with that good health intact requires a combined effort of adaptation, homeostasis, instinct, and wise actions.

Concepts of good health vary greatly. It is essentially a measure of our being able to do what we want to do and becoming what we want to become. Good health also implies our success in functioning within our particular set of values; thus, health has considerable variation. On the one hand, a middle-aged man with a previous heart attack may consider himself healthy if he is able to work as an accountant each day. On the other hand, a young, hard-driving former football player considers himself healthy if he can play racquetball fiercely two hours without tiring. The maintenance of good health depends on how we live and the confidence with which we face the dangers of the environment. The hostility of the environment would be more threatening were it not for those factors which guarantee us certain but not complete success in adapting to its challenges.

Consider the threat to the wild animals living in certain areas of East Africa and compare their environmental dangers to those of your own. I have been privileged to drive to the rim of the Ngorongoro Crater in Tanzania and search the crater floor for the beautiful zebra, giraffe, impala, wildebeest, lion, and elephant. The scene appears tranquil, but the snoozing of the lion is interrupted by hunger, and the survival-of-the-fittest struggle erupts with a wild flight to safety by his intended prey. These animals are particularly fitted to live in this sort of environment. The characteristics of their anatomy and physiology are passed to their offspring, and their cycle of life is played out for them—interrupted only by man's presence.

There are important differences between the abilities of these animals to adapt to their environment and our ability to adapt to ours. In the first place, most animals are limited by their anatomy and physiology to a narrow range of activities. They are more specialized than we. They may run or climb, but few have the ability to perform such a wide range of actions as we—climbing, running, crawling, walking, swimming, sitting, and others. Secondly, these animals, born, living, and dying in that same area, are unlike man for he has truly inhabited the earth.

The air is too thin for our lungs but the Sherpa guide on the slopes of the Himalaya Mountains at 12,000-plus feet has adapted to it. The Jordanians living 1,300 feet below sea level near the Dead Sea adapt to different circumstances; both, however, accentuate the differences humans can tolerate. In moving about the world, establishing colonies here, there, and everywhere, man has adapted to changed weather, climate, and food. Our modifications of nature, though, may cause unpredictable consequences for our environment and our health.

Life gets boring if we don't have new experiences—our personalities become dull and uninteresting. Consequently, we seek the excitement of the unknown, the challenge of the uncharted. These pursuits thrust us into circumstances which suit us poorly. We are not biologically or socially well adapted to every situation to which we are exposed, but the quest goes on, for life is dull without excitement.

Travelers during the Renaissance period were just as excited by new experiences and new places, but they were not prepared for the sickness and death visited upon them by bubonic plague and other infections. Travel became more commonplace during the Industrial Revolution, and many forsook the peaceful rural life for the glamor of the cities. Instead of the promise of a new life, many found themselves afflicted with tuberculosis and other diseases as they crowded together in miserable tenement houses. We have conquered sewage disposal and purified our water and food, but our modern technologies and prosperity are, in part, the cause of many of our diseases today—heart trouble, high blood pressure, diabetes, stroke, cancer, and personality disorders.

We have more than one environment which may affect our health. We usually think of the effects of our water, air, and countryside, but this is only a part of the picture. We have an environment of relationships which may affect our health—the effect of people on people—our family members, friends, acquaintances, and strangers. Chemicals may poison our air, water, and land; we may counteract or cleanse the chemical, or if exposed, react with an illness. Our environment of relationships can also make us sick. The sight of a food may cause nausea if our previous association with that food was marked by the memory of something unpleasant. The sight of a friend, with whom we are at odds, may cause a quickened pulse, a blush, sweaty hands, and the like. The end of a love relationship may awaken a healed peptic ulcer. Fear about the successful conclusion of a business deal may cause an irregular heart beat, a tightness in the chest, and sweating of the palms.

Our health then has far more complexity than that of the animals living at the base of the Ngorongoro Crater. We survive because we have been able to adapt to different living conditions, as well as having been born with certain protective mechanisms which are God-given. We are able to do a great many things because of the way our bodies are built and the way they work. But we have also had to adapt to different foods. There are many different eating patterns in the world—some people are nourished primarily by meat, others by vegetables, and yet others a combination of meat and vegetables to survive. The human body adapts quite well to these different foods.

Adaptation in different environments is far from perfect. For example, the Sherpa has adapted to the thinner air by producing more red blood cells which carry more oxygen. His body, however, has no effective means of shutting off the production of these cells by the bone marrow. He may thus produce too many cells, his blood becoming too thick, causing a disease known as chronic mountain sickness. Thus, the adaptation process is not finely tuned.

We are even able to adapt to horrible changes in life as shown by certain examples from the history of our modern age. Consider how millions of people were exposed to the unspeakable horror of the trenches of World War I, the ordeals of the bestial atmosphere of concentration camps, the sophisticated but devastating weapons of World War II, the Korean, and Vietnam wars. Yet they were able to survive and largely to recover and have useful lives.

Even today, for reasons which are hard to understand, we see people of all ages and races moving to polluted, traumatic lives in crowded cities. Rapid growth of large cities brings living conditions so distasteful as to seem incompatible with life. Yet, these circumstances demonstrate in some degree our ability to adjust to pollution, poor diets, and ghetto crowding, as well as to monotony and ugly surroundings.

Some of our adjustments to the environmental problems caused by modern civilization are bought at a high price. Smoke and fumes spoil the air around us. Fish can hardly live in the filth in our streams, lakes, and oceans. Noise, glaring lights, and other excessive, unnatural stimulation keep our nervous systems on edge and contribute to the patterns of disease which we experience. It is highly likely that we have more heart trouble, more cancer, more trouble getting along with other people, and more chronic, degenerative disease, not because we live longer, but because we live crowded, highly pressured lives.

Are we born with an ability to adapt to such things as air pollution, resulting from industry and automobile usage? The answer is yes, but the adaptation is not perfect and, in truth, may be destructive. For example, repeated exposure to cigarette smoke, irritating industrial fumes, or heavy concentrations of automobile exhaust will irritate our bronchial tubes. The bronchial mucus cells pour out more mucus to protect delicate lung tissue from these irritants. This excessive mucus causes coughs, shortness of breath, and the onset of bronchitis and emphysema.

A similar example of imperfect adaptation is noted when workers in noisy plants become hard of hearing. The body adapts to the noise by reducing the ability to hear, but the consequence of this is that our ability to hear our friends' conversations is reduced and musical tones are not heard as well.

In still another example of excessive stimulation we learn that we have limits to the number of problems we can face and solve each day. When we must listen to many people, each with different troubles, we may respond as though we don't care, and as a consequence, see feelings hurt. This is true in family relations but is a special problem for those involved in counseling or caring professional work.

We don't adapt as well to some modern diseases as we do to changes in climate, different foods, or weather. There is no adaptation to cancer of the lung as a result of cigarette smoking. Most people with this problem have the diagnosis made after their children are born; so it can't be prevented by inheritance. The child whose father is crippled and dies from this disease has as great a chance of getting the same disease if he smokes. Genetic adaptation, even if it will work, is a very slow process, usually taking generations before an effect is seen.

WHY DO WE BECOME ILL?

The environment has more threats to our health than we have abilities to resist. We cannot adapt to every threat. The nature of the danger, and our ability or inability to resist it, will be the deciding factor in whether we become ill or develop a form of tolerance which results in a body that doesn't work as well as it once did. We may be threatened by dangers which are not related to our actions; we may be innocent bystanders. For example, a mudslide or flood at night may sweep away homes and lives; a tank car of chlorine gas may derail with escaping gas damaging the lungs of those nearby. On the other hand, God has set the universe in motion with laws of nature providing balance and orderliness. Ignoring or attempting to abridge these laws may result in injury or sickness. If we become drunk from alcohol and ram the car against a bridge abutment, we will likely be injured or die. The poisonous tars from cigarette smoke will damage lungs and cause cancer, bronchitis, or emphysema. In these examples we are not innocent bystanders, but are part of the cause—the disease or injury is the effect.

Ancient physicians, long before the Christian era, were concerned about the effects of climate and living conditions as they relate to health and disease. Alcmaeon of Croton and Empedocles of ancient Greece defined health as being in harmony with the universe and disease as a state of imbalance. Medical writers of early days supported this popular view, but absurd notions grew out of it. For example, in the Middle Ages the stars and planets were emphasized and physicians studied their patients' horoscopes with as much care as the modern physician studies his patient's electrocardiogram.

This concept of balance with the environment was to take shape gradually. However, our knowledge of the body's use of food as the source of energy and our knowledge of the body's chemical processes had to develop before a French physiologist, Claude Bernard, could advance the idea that the internal environment of the body is protected from damage by remaining relatively constant.

HOMEOSTASIS

Dr. Bernard felt that we survive and stay healthy because our internal fluids, blood plasma and lymph, stay the same, despite the foods we eat or the changes in weather or differences in climate. Though Dr. Bernard knew this to be true, he could not demonstrate it scientifically. Many years passed before scientific advances would identify the way the body stays in dynamic balance. Dr. Walter Cannon, a Harvard University physiologist, introduced the word *homeostasis* in explaining the continuous adjustment the body makes to keep its internal composition within safe limits.

Although this is another way we survive despite change, this is not a perfect system. For example, my chain saw might slip, cutting my leg deeply enough to cause a severe hemorrhage and a drop in blood pressure. Instantly the body senses the drop in pressure due to the loss of blood and, in an effort to protect the heart, the brain, kidneys, and lungs make several adjustments. In the first few minutes the arteries to the muscles and skin become smaller, shifting their blood supply to more vital areas. The heart beats faster and breathing becomes faster in an attempt to carry more oxygen to the brain. But the process is not selective enough. Even though the arteries to muscle and skin become smaller in an effort to protect other organs, some damage to these more vital organs can occur. The arteries become smaller through chemicals, and these same chemicals cause the arteries to the kidneys to become smaller, even though the body wishes to protect the kidneys. Consequently, the process may result in damage to the kidneys, but life may be saved.

It is probably true, but hard to prove, that we have a balance system which comes into play when we are exposed to more stress than we can reasonably bear. We may then be provoked to anger or excitement over minor things. If this anger or excitement persists or grows worse, it may become a serious form of abnormal behavior—an obsession or maniacal state.

The mechanisms of homeostasis help ensure survival, but this wisdom is not finely tuned and as a result of a homeostatic reaction, we could later develop a disease with fatal consequences.

INSTINCT

We essentially respond to immediate danger in the environment by instinct. Instincts are a result of our experiences, but if experiences are limited, our instincts are of little help in solving "life's way." If a new danger looms before us, for example, radiation exposure that is invisible or chemical fumes that are odorless, our instincts are powerless to warn us of the peril, much less show us the avenue to escape. Instinct has low value in guaranteeing our survival from environmental threats.

WISDOM

Adaptation grants us flexibility to live in almost every part of the world under different climates, eating different kinds of food, but it is powerless to prevent diseases of modern civilization. Homeostasis has its limitations. Instincts would be more useful if the world stayed the same, but we live in a changing world where our minds are stirred alive as we gain knowledge and are motivated to satisfy our yearning for adventure and creativity. These yearnings for adventure may carry us beyond the limits of safety. We are able to direct adaptation at this point and make choices which, in part, assure our survival. Since the instinctual and homeostatic wisdom of the body are blind and sometimes faulty, we must substitute for it a wisdom based on knowledge of present conditions and anticipation of future consequences.

If we are to stay well and avoid sickness, we must make choices about our habits and the circumstances in which we live. Our health depends largely on our selection of a life-style and our adaptation to its experiences and problems. Sickness, of one type or another, will come to all of us, but certain kinds of sickness are delayed or prevented by our choices of life-style. Even when sickness develops we usually have enough knowledge to evaluate our circumstances and decide on a course of action designed to correct the problems, either alone or with proper help.

Any form of physical and mental disease disrupts life and is to be regarded as evil. Our plans and goals in life are interrupted. This interference amounts to a loss of freedom. We hope to recover this freedom when we visit the doctor. The physician, however, may not have a cure; he may only be able to arrest the disease. Thus, we live but the body functions at a new level—a lower level. On the other hand, healing may not be possible, and our adaptive and homeostatic functions falter and ultimately fail. We may then harbor resentment because the disease cannot be halted or harbor fear of death as the problems mount. The pain of the disease process further depresses our spirits, and we wonder whether God is interested in our plight.

I believe that we have a spiritual homeostasis just as we do an internal, physical one. We may drift along, living life in a casual manner with few troubles but with a vague feeling of uneasiness or unfulfillment. Things are not quite right but we can't put our fingers on the trouble. I believe this feeling of uneasiness is an indication of our innate sense of God and of the need to strengthen that relationship with God. The coolness of the relationship dawns when a crisis arises—we seek God as we cry out for help. Spiritual homeostasis indicates our need to reinforce our relationship with the Great Physician. This is different from our internal homeostasis; our bodies respond internally without our knowledge, largely unconscious, whereas our response in fulfilling our spiritual need is altogether within our will, entirely conscious. The choice is open. We respond as we will.

When death is approaching painfully, fiercesomely, and perhaps grotesquely, I feel powerless to prevent it—what then? Beyond the unknown and the pain, I feel the reassurance of a bright new world that will erase the tears and memories of the hurt. I believe that Jesus is the Great Physician who is grieved by the pain of his believers' suffering, but that knowing him is worth the enduring. He may have used the sickness to teach us and let it turn us to him. He has created a new world and pain shall be no more.

> Listen, I tell you a mystery: We will not all
> sleep, but we shall all be changed—in a flash,
> in the twinkling of an eye, at the last trumpet.
> For the trumpet will sound, the dead will be
> raised imperishable, and we shall be changed.
> For the perishable must clothe itself with the
> imperishable, and the mortal with immortality.
> When the perishable has been clothed with the
> imperishable and the mortal with immortality,

then the saying that is written will come true:
"Death has been swallowed up in Victory.
Where, O death, is your Victory?
Where, O death, is your sting?"
                              (1 Cor. 15:51-55, NIV)

2
The Diseased Heart

Keep thy heart with all diligence; for out of it are the issues of life (Prov. 4:23).

A sound heart is the life of the flesh (Prov. 14:30).

CASE HISTORY

Joe Thompkins, a forty-three-year-old retired Navy man, suddenly grabbed his chest and slumped from his chair to the floor while eating the evening meal with his wife and eleven-year-old son. His son had watched a television program on cardiopulmonary resuscitation three weeks before, and also knew that his father had experienced a previous heart attack.

He sensed the urgency of the moment, told his mother to call the Rescue Squad, turned his father onto his back, checked the mouth for obstruction, flexed his father's neck and started mouth-to-mouth resuscitation. He gave his father two breaths and started chest massage. The mother returned and took over the mouth-to-mouth breathing as the son continued the chest massage. The father stirred within five minutes and breathed on his own within ten minutes. His condition improved but was complicated by shock. His blood pressure fell to 90/60 and his skin became cold and clammy.

The Rescue Squad, upon arrival, started an IV of 5 percent dextrose in water along with oxygen at 10 liters a minute. His condition stabilized, his color improved, and his blood pressure rose to 112/74 within ten minutes. He was then swiftly transported ten miles to the local hospital with entry by way of the emergency department. The nurse promptly notified the doctor of his arrival. An EKG was ordered, morphine was administered for pain, and he was transferred to a hospital bed. Oxygen was continued at 10 liters and the IV slowed to a drip. His blood pressure and pulse were stable. The EKG showed an extensive heart attack of the bottom of the heart. He was transferred to the coronary care unit.

At the age of thirty-nine, the patient had undergone the first attack of chest pain while on reserve duty at a distant naval base. He was hospitalized for three weeks with a diagnosis of an anterior heart attack. His course in the naval hospital had been complicated by a disturbance of heart rhythm requiring electric shock. Upon discharge from the Navy, he continued his work as a draftsman for an architect. He was strongly advised to quit his habit of smoking two packs of cigarettes daily and to begin a program of exercise. He did neither. His cholesterol was usually over 250 mg. percent. His blood pressure was usually 180/110 even though he was on blood pressure medicines, and he was eighty pounds overweight.

This type of case history is heard daily in hundreds of hospitals in our country—a young man with a critical illness which will cripple him if it doesn't kill him. He, unable to act on the doctor's advice, continued to smoke. Additionally he ate too much and exercised too little. His bad habits controlled him. This is an example of the threat of sedentary living in an affluent society, coupled with exposure to substances harmful to the body's internal environment (cigarette smoke).

We think of Joe's problem—atherosclerosis (commonly called hardening of the arteries)—as a modern-day scourge! It is, but only in that it affects so many people in the modern world. It has actually been found in the mummies of Egyptian tombs and the word comes from the Greek word, *athere,* which means gruel, a thin, watery porridge. Atherosclerosis has been known for a long time but in some ways it remains a mystery. We do know that it causes such problems as coronary heart disease (the cause of Joe's attack), strokes, and other vascular problems.

If Joe had lived in Kenya, East Africa, among the Masai tribe, he would have occupied his time with herding the cattle, walking long distances, playing war games, and dancing Masai dances. He would have eaten differently as well. The main difference would be in the amount of fat. The Masai eat 10 percent fat, except in the rainy season when they drink large amounts of milk mixed with the blood of their cattle. We eat an average of 42 percent fat in our diets. Even with the high cholesterol and fat levels contained in the milk, the Masai don't get hardening of the arteries. This is so unusual that a number of scientists have tried to explain it.

Since we get part of our cholesterol from our foods and part produced within the body, it has been proposed that the Masai have a different cutoff mechanism that stops the body's production when they drink the increased milk during the rainy season. If and how this works is not known. Dr. George Mann of Vanderbilt University believes that the milk the Masai drink is different from that which we drink. It is true that they allow it to ferment before drinking it—this fermentation produces yogurt. So Dr. Mann feels a "yogurt factor" lowers the Masai cholesterol level.

Whatever the reason, the fact is well known that in Africa, New Guinea, Ecuador, and other less-developed countries, people don't have the same problems with atherosclerosis, heart trouble, and strokes as people in countries with more sedentary life-styles. We recognize that this is true and that improper diet and insufficient physical activity seem to play a major role in vascular disease.

Joe's disease is easily studied with the electrocardiogram, blood tests, and X-ray. The severity of his heart attack, as well as the amount of muscle damage, can be accurately determined. It is possible to inject a dye into the arteries of the heart and note the narrow area of blockage caused by the cholesterol in the wall. All of this, however, doesn't reveal the basic cause of his trouble.

If Joe dies, an autopsy can study the heart and artery damage in minute detail, but even this tells nothing of how the disease developed. We do realize that many soldiers in their early twenties who died from injuries in the Korean and Vietnam wars had diseased arteries. Even children who died from accidents often have some evidence of hardening of the arteries. It is a disease of silence which cuts people down in their most productive years though beginning in childhood.

Five thousand, two hundred and nine men and women, some in

good health and others with problems similar to Joe's, have been studied over the past twenty-five years at Framingham, Massachusetts. We have learned enough to recognize that some habits increase the risks of coronary heart disease and that these risks can be lessened.

Joe's cholesterol was about 250 mg. This is too high. Excess cholesterol in the blood will enter the cells lining the walls of our arteries, forming a "fatty streak." This may get larger and larger, forming new minute blood vessels and developing a thick cover, becoming known then as a "fibrous plaque." These two basic changes are made worse by certain bad factors—cigarette smoking, eating too much fat, gaining too much weight, living too easy a life, and hypertension.

Of course, as was the case in Joe's attack, the "fibrous plaque" slows the flow of blood, causing a blood clot! This may block the artery at that point or flow to another area where it lodges. This blockage of blood flow starves the wall of the heart, if in a coronary artery, or starves the brain if in a carotid artery. On the one hand, a heart attack results—on the other, a stroke is the outcome.

Risk Factors

Joe had certain risks which he knew about but did nothing to minimize—others were beyond his control.

1. *Maleness.* For some unknown reason, men have three times the risk of women in developing heart trouble before the age of sixty. This seems to be related to female hormones because a woman who reaches the age of menopause loses this protection. Stranger yet is the fact that a woman married to a man who has had a heart attack will have a greater risk of developing coronary heart disease. This suggests that something they both do or fail to do may be involved, perhaps their diets, or lack of exercise.

2. *Physical Activity.* Joe's job as a draftsman involved sitting over a drawing board most of the day. In the evenings he was too tired to do anything more than sit in front of the TV set, munching and smoking. The Framingham Study points out the benefits of an active life. In the active group, there was less likelihood of a heart attack and if one occurred, it was less likely to be fatal. Surprisingly, this

was of as significant importance in the elderly. Staying active is vital for older people. People who had fast pulses and shortness of breath on slight activity or were overweight were usually in poor condition.

3. *Diabetes.* Glucose makes the body run, and the brain work, but if the blood sugar becomes too high because of insufficient insulin levels, we have diabetes. Diabetes is present in one of every twenty persons, but those who develop it in adolescence or in their twenties have so-called juvenile diabetes. This type almost always requires insulin but the adult type, occurring after age thirty, may require only diet or oral medications, though sometimes insulin is necessary.

Diabetes will more likely occur if: (1) someone in the family has diabetes; (2) you weigh too much (85 percent of adult diabetes occurs in overweight people); (3) you are thirty-five years or older; (4) you are the mother of a large infant. Diabetes increases the risk of heart disease and stroke but we don't fully understand the reason. The chances of death from a heart attack are doubled. Weakness of the heart wall with heart failure develops in women with diabetes. Fairly strict control of the diabetes, keeping the blood sugars as close to normal as possible, is of benefit in preventing these complications.

4. *Hypertension—High Blood Pressure.* Joe's blood pressure was 180/110 even though he took medications for controlling it. This is one of the problems facing the 25 to 30 million Americans who have high blood pressure. Many have it but don't know it, and others know it but are not well controlled in spite of taking medicines. It is a deadly, largely silent killer affecting the arteries of the heart, kidneys, and brain.

A thirty-five-year-old man with a blood pressure of 150/110 will run the risk of dying sixteen years earlier than his friends of similar age with a normal blood pressure. If he smokes, as did Joe, and if his cholesterol is elevated, as was Joe's, his chances of a heart attack are four times that of a normal person, and chances of a stroke are seven times that of a normal person!

Terms relating to hypertension are sometimes confusing. High blood pressure and hypertension mean the same—too much pressure on the walls of the arteries. The blood is under normal pressure as the heart pushes it forward but if too high, the arterial walls change from smooth, spaghetti-like, flexible tubes to knobby, rigid tubes similar to rusty pipes.

Emotions, weight, diet (especially too much salt), and kidney disease play a role in hypertension. Nervous tension is sometimes confused with hypertension, but even a calm person can have high blood pressure, and jobs of considerable stress don't necessarily produce hypertension. Some people are intense and hard-driving while others are phlegmatic. Classifications of temperament are not consistently useful in predicting high blood pressure.

As the nurse or doctor listens over the artery in your arm when your blood pressure is taken, there is more than one sound. As the blood is forced from the heart, it advances as a column, reaching a certain height and then falling away. The pressure *at its highest point* makes a certain sound and is recorded as the systolic pressure. As it falls away, the flow within the artery becomes silent. This point is recorded as the diastolic pressure. This represents the end of the cycle; the heart is filled ready to start a new cycle again and again, 60-100 times per minute.

This problem of hypertension has been publicized with warnings to have your blood pressure checked. That's good advice. Blood pressure screening at health clinics or special clinics will alert you to the need of further checking. Your blood pressure will vary from time to time and the best, most practical indicator of the need for treatment is an average of several readings, taken at a doctor's office. After all, we have learned from several studies that bringing blood pressure to almost normal levels is life-saving, but this is usually a commitment to lifelong taking of medicines. You will want to be sure you need them.

5. *Smoking.* Most everyone knows that smoking is bad for health. Doctors, dentists, and pharmacists believe it—many have quit. Women and teenagers must feel that it is the "in thing" to do to live dangerously exciting lives, because the number of those smoking has increased. The tobacco ads push a sexy image or one seeking relaxation through lighting up. The reasons for smoking are as unclear as the understanding of human nature. But what is known is the strength of the habit that cigarettes have if you smoke. The idea

THE DISEASED HEART

of a "nicotine fit" is fairly close to the truth. Smokers develop psychological, as well as physical, dependence on nicotine. This makes it hard to quit.

Joe knew the advantage of quitting smoking but was never able to do it. For him, just as for millions of other Americans, this is one of the most harmful personal habits. Every time he "lit up" he increased the risk of:

Lung Cancer: Heavy smokers are twenty-four times more likely to develop lung cancer than nonsmokers. In 1976, 68,000 Americans lost their lives from cancer of the lungs caused by smoking. In addition, one may develop cancer of the mouth, lips, vocal cords, pancreas, and bladder.

Emphysema: One of the saddest sights in medicine is to view the person, previously strong and able, now huffing and puffing even as he sits resting. To walk across the room is torture because his breath is too short. Almost every heavy smoker will develop some degree of this trouble, and during his final years of life the threat of death from respiratory failure hangs over him like a sword.

Heart Attacks: Smoking mothers are twice as likely to have a spontaneous miscarriage. If a miscarriage doesn't occur, the baby is usually of lighter weight and has an increased risk of bronchitis or pneumonia during its first year of life.

Wrinkles: Women who smoke have more facial wrinkles than nonsmokers. This may convince those who worry more about how they look than about how they feel to give up smoking.

Money Problems: If you smoke two packs a day for one year, you could have bought two tailor-made suits or spent a week at a resort.

Other: Food doesn't smell or taste as good, and an irritating cough may develop. You could cause a fire in bed if you smoke there, either burning the house down or killing yourself. Smokers have bad breath and tobacco odor in their homes, cars, and offices. If you quit, smell and taste improve and cough lessens in a few days. Shortness of breath improves in a few weeks and if you stay off cigarettes long enough (several years) your risk of lung cancer and heart attack returns to the same as a nonsmoker.

6. *Diet, Cholesterol, and Weight.* The way we eat and the development of a diseased heart are related to each other but cigarette

smoking, high blood pressure, and lack of exercise are interrelated. Even if the blood-pressure problem is solved with medicines and we begin exercising and quit smoking, we still must consider the role of the food we eat. Cholesterol is the part of our diet which has received the most attention, when considering the causes of heart disease. This stems from experiments in which animals are fed cholesterol and develop heart disease as a result. Animal experiments raise suspicion about cholesterol, but there is a problem when trying to supply animal information to humans.

Consider the difference in heart attack rates between men in Finland as compared to those in Japan. The diet in Finland is richer in dairy products and red meats with fewer vegetables. The Japanese eat more vegetables and fish but fewer dairy products and less red meat. The men in Finland have higher blood cholesterol levels and have a chance of developing a heart attack that is ten times as great as that for Japanese men who have low blood cholesterol levels.

Most scientists believe that eating food which raises cholesterol levels is a cause of coronary heart disease. Dr. Kaare Norum of the University of Oslo, Norway, questioned 214 scientists and 99 percent agreed that fatty foods raise cholesterol levels, and that elevated cholesterol is an indication of increased risk of developing heart disease. Surprisingly, the cholesterol-containing foods are not the major problems. Even more important is the amount of fat we eat. Fat makes food taste better, and we like the taste more than we like to trim the fat from the border of a steak or pork chop. Some fats are more harmful than others; fat from red meat, such as beef, is more harmful than that from chicken. Chicken fat is more harmful than that from fish. Most vegetables have a soft fat (polyunsaturated) and this accounts for the promotion of vegetable fats for cooking oils or in making mayonnaise for sandwiches or salads.

Cholesterol is not all bad. It is everywhere within the body—within each cell. Cortisone, sex hormones, and bile hormones are made from it; it participates in many body functions. We cannot live without it.

Recently we have learned an important new fact about cholesterol. It was puzzling in the past that some people with high cholesterol levels didn't develop heart disease, and some people with low levels did develop heart disease. Now it seems that there are two types of cholesterol: (1) a helpful cholesterol called HDL (High Density Lipoprotein) and (2) a harmful cholesterol called LDL (Low Density Lipoprotein).

Surprisingly, if there is a high level of HDL, the heart attack rate drops. Women have more HDL than men—perhaps the reason they have fewer heart attacks. LDL seems to carry fatty substances to the walls of the arteries, looks for an injured cell, and lays one layer on top of another until a plaque is formed. HDL, on the other hand, protects arteries by removing fatty materials from the layers of the plaque. If HDL is beneficial, can we build or increase our levels of HDL? The answer is yes, and here's how:

1. *Change your diet.* Eat more vegetables, cereals, fish, less red meat, and no foods such as hot dogs or potato chips, which are packed with hard fats.
2. *Quit smoking.* People who smoke have low HDL and former smokers, having quit for one year or longer, will have regained normal HDL levels.
3. *Exercise.* Dr. Pete D. Wood of Stanford University checked forty-one very active men who run at least fifteen miles per week and compared them to inactive men of the same ages. The runners had a cholesterol level of 200 mgs.; but the non-runners were only slightly higher at 210 mgs.; however, the runners had a much higher HDL level. Other studies have confirmed this finding.
4. *Weight.* It is clear that the person twenty to thirty pounds overweight has a greater risk of heart attacks. It seems that young men have a higher risk than women. Diabetes, high blood pressure, or cigarette smoking changes the picture. Increased weight becomes a more serious health problem if these are present.
5. *Sugars.* Sugars cause dental caries and pile up the pounds of weight, but are not thought to be primarily related to heart disease.

6. *Coffee.* Coffee has not proven to be a risk factor but most smokers are heavy coffee drinkers and this, in part, is the reason some studies are confusing.

Most studies conclude that coronary heart disease is due to more than one cause, and the multiple causes are then aggravated by other factors. The most important factors are aging, high blood pressure, cigarette smoking, and cholesterol. The person who smokes, has uncontrolled blood pressure, and an elevated cholesterol level has a risk of having a heart attack that is over eight times that of a person who has normal blood pressure, normal cholesterol, and doesn't smoke.

Now let's return to Joe Thompkins. Joe continued to improve from his attack, returning home three weeks after admission to the hospital. In spite of his family's joy at his homecoming, he couldn't seem to get on top of his gloomy feelings. Everything was so much effort. Tiredness overcame him when he read the paper, walked to the table, or sat watching TV. There was no joy in his heart. He started to walk out of doors but his chest hurt if he walked fast. Three months passed and he didn't feel well enough to return to work. He was referred to a nearby medical center for studies to determine if an operation could improve the flow of blood to the wall of his heart.

At the Medical Center, a tube was passed through a vein into the heart chamber. A movie taken, when dye was injected into the arteries supplying blood to the wall of the heart, showed extensive damage to each of the three major arteries. The conclusion: an operation would be too risky.

Joe's spirits sank even lower. He had no interest in life, preferring to stay in bed most of the day. He felt more heartsick than sick with heart disease. He became introspective, searching his life for meaning, berating himself for his inability to be a father and breadwinner.

Joe's heart problem is severe but reasonably stable. His depression complicates his condition. He needs a source of hope. Medicine has no cure for his condition.

Joe, not yet old in years, has a heart too weak to sustain him. His hope of recovery is realistically nonexistent, and his hopelessness now becomes his major problem. In seeking Joe's healing as a whole person, the doctor may sense his spiritual need and serve it with patience, interest, God-given love, and psychological skill.

3
Human Nature—Worried Sick

But the Lord answered and said to her, "Martha, Martha, you are worried and bothered about so many things; but only a few things are necessary, really only one, for Mary has chosen the good part, which shall not be taken away from her" (Luke 10:41,42, NASB).

A common theme running throughout the criticisms of our health-care system is the charge of inadequacy or insufficiency. Some of the criticisms are: It's hard to get an appointment with the doctor; doctors don't have sufficient time or interest to see everyone; there's too little money, too little commitment.

And yet, the health system has expanded with great vigor in the past twenty-five years. It has been a growth industry. In 1950, our total expenditures to health care were $10 billion. By 1972, it had risen to $70 billion. In 1974, it was $110 billion. In 1977, it exceeded $130 billion, and it is expected to reach close to $300 billion in 1990. The role of inflation and population growth can account for some of these increases, but a major change has occurred since 1950. Has our health disintegrated, requiring billions of dollars in new resources to meet the crisis? Has our technology advanced so rapidly that our handling of health problems has undergone a major transformation? There is no real evidence that health in general has deteriorated to the extent indicated by the new dollars spent each year for health care. On the contrary, we seem to have gotten along reasonably well with a few notable exceptions.

A major change over the past twenty-five years is our loss of confidence in the healthy condition of our bodies. This has led to the general belief of a fundamental flaw in our bodies, subject to immediate disintegration or always on the very edge of mortal disease.

Many visits by doctors are made for evaluation and reassurance for these "worried sick." Television programs and commercials, magazines and newspaper articles reinforce our need for shoring up our personal health. Some "worried sick" patients seek reassurance from the doctor for imagined diseases triggered by family, economic, or other social problems. Others have worried over the doctor's diagnosis of a chronic or a serious disease.

The increased patient visits are made most often to family physicians and internists, the former receiving 234 million visits or 41.3 percent of the total office visits to physicians for a wide variety of reasons—for symptoms of sickness, as well as for examinations to assure wellness. Chest pains, problems of the legs and feet, fatigue, abdominal pain, high blood pressure, coughs, and stomach upsets were frequent symptoms. Diseases of the circulatory system, such as heart disease, hypertension, and stroke, accounted for one fourth of all visits made to internists. Diabetes, colds, flu-like illnesses, and emotional problems were also frequently diagnosed. Most of these visits were for chronic illness, and this tendency toward chronic conditions increased with the increasing age of patients.

Sickness, doctors, and medicine are frequent topics of conversation in many gatherings. Our concern for health is very high on our list of values but much illness is not even cared for by doctors. It is estimated that 70-90 percent of all self-recognized episodes of sickness are taken care of by self-treatment, family care, self-help groups, religious practitioners, and other types of healers. This portrays the role of faith in seeking healing.

Doctors are able to diagnose the cause of a patient's problem in a very high percentage of cases. Diseases of the heart, of the muscles, and of the brain are classified in an orderly fashion. Much knowledge has accumulated to explain almost every disease that causes trouble in humans, except for one area. We do not know a great deal about the effect of the mind on the body's reactions. The mind plays tricks on the body. We may fear that we have a disease and visit the doctors for an examination to confirm that fear or reassure us that nothing is wrong. This fear of a disease, and the anxiousness that accompanies it, is a form of suffering, just as despair, loneliness, or heart trouble cause suffering.

Suffering caused by despair, loneliness, or fear may cause symptoms which mimic many diseases. The doctor's exam fails to disclose a disease (30 to 45 percent of visits to the doctor are for problems for which no cause can be found) or a disease may be found and cured, but we still feel sick. Moreover, the suggested or prescribed treatment may fail to cure the problem, despite a medicine that is prescribed specifically for the condition.

PATTERNS OF SICKNESS

There is much support for the idea that disease and sickness are different. On the one hand, disease is a malfunction or failure of a part of the body or mind. Sickness, on the other hand, represents how we feel and how our friends and families feel about our not being quite as well as usual. Our family backgrounds, or circle of friends, our religious backgrounds will shape the way we tell about, explain, or label a period during which we are unwell.

Sickness will affect each of us differently, and our behavior will be individualized. A person of considerable education, for example, will interpret the doctor's explanations differently than a tenant farmer will. The doctor's explanation and method of communicating depends on his background, his value system, and his personality. The doctor who believes in a living God and maintains a personal relationship to him through Jesus Christ will have a different value system than the doctor who is an agnostic. The first will view life from his belief of eternal life through Jesus, and the latter will likely see life as ending with death. When a doctor tries to console and give hope to a dying man and his family, the event will have different meanings for the Christian and non-Christian doctor. The patient who is dying but knows Jesus and has eternal life is different from the patient dying without that hope.

Pain is a part of many diseases. I recently treated a young mother who had abdominal pain due to gall bladder colic following the delivery of her baby. She was unable to care for her new baby. The pain's severity caused her not only a disruption of her daily routine, but a feeling of depression. The pain, a signal alerting her to the need of help, was beneficial in one way but was also an unwanted change in her life.

Another of my patients, a young lady, developed symptoms of a peptic ulcer. Her ulcer, though in her stomach, erupted as a result of an emotional entanglement. Bit by bit the story unfolded. She had become friendly with a fellow worker at her place of employment, a furniture plant. This friendliness grew until it ended with sexual relations. She feared pregnancy and examination confirmed it. This marked the beginning of a lifetime of illness. Her ulcer persisted, unyielding to therapy. Palpitations, high blood pressure, and severe headaches developed. Her life of sickness rested on a foundation of doubt, guilt, fear, anxiety, and depression. Two daughters from her marriage were in their teens when she delivered the child from this pregnancy. The older children, using drugs and alcohol, lived unruly, undisciplined lives. The patient's father, an alcoholic for many years, died of cirrhosis of the liver.

THE ROOTS OF ANXIETY AND DEPRESSION

After spending a lifetime distinguishing himself as a master diagnostician, Dr. Walter Alvarez, in 1958, wrote a book entitled *Practical Leads to Puzzling Diagnoses*. In his studies, Dr. Alvarez probed the backgrounds of families for clues to explain alcoholism, mental retardation, epilepsy, odd behavior, depression, eccentricity, anxiety, and many psychosomatic illnesses. He concluded after analyzing hundreds of records that a strong hereditary link existed in family members who showed a tendency to emotional illness. This tendency, however, could develop into different diseases.

Dr. Alvarez, as an example, gave the lineage of the Royal Family of Spain. A small streak of madness was inherited through the descendants of "Joanna the Mad," a daughter of King Ferdinand and Queen Isabella. The Spaniards nicknamed these descendants "Luis the Weak," "Luis the Foolish," "Maria the Licentious," "Philip the Imbecile," "Maria Luisa the Stupid," "Frances the Bigoted," "Carlotta the Violent," "Ferdinand the Brutal," "Balthasar the Degenerate," and "Philip the Lazy."

For several years, I have participated in a spring retreat for the class of a children's home. Most of these youngsters are wards of the courts or social service departments. They have been removed from a home made intolerable by violence, drugs, alcohol, or moral failure. They are not abandoned as hopeless because of their background of undesirable environmental influence. These children, though from a miserable home situation, are as likely to become good and sensible citizens as they are to follow a life of grief. If they, as they mature, follow a life of grief, it may well be that the difference in their reaction to the environment depends upon inheriting a good or poor nervous system from one of the parents. Their reaction to life is likely to reflect their interpretation of life from their past experiences.

THE SHAPING OF OUR MINDS

For centuries men have tried to understand mankind with such terms as the classical view of man, the Christian view of man, the Renaissance view of man, or even the Chinese view of man. It is still a complex subject with a great deal of confusion and a babble of voices. Writers on the subject have been thoughtful men, but unfortunately we have more often been so busy reading detective stories, the comics, *Playboy,* or sports magazines that the writings of thoughtful men are not read. These other pieces of literature plus television do much to pervade our homes and minds with great influence as we develop our systems of values and ideas. Writings such as these named are available all over the world, and a wide variety of impressions are gained from them.

Starting in the late 1940s, Micky Spillane has written one book after another with the same theme. His heroes have mocked and swaggered across the boundaries of both statutory and moral law. Mayhem, assault, and murder have been brutally carried out in those pages. The hero sat in personal judgment above other people—his character immoral, his ideas evil, and his punishment sadistic. Yet he regarded his brutal actions as justifiable means to an admirable end.

Spillane's hero and his view of life are to be contrasted with that of Agatha Christie's Hercule Poirot. Poirot is gentle, fond of people, and on the side of law and justice. Another pair of contrasts are James Bond and Sherlock Holmes. They represent two outlooks on life, both committed to combating evil but in different ways. The world of Poirot and Holmes are logically constructed and can be reasoned out. They eventually unearth the secrets of crime. On the other hand, the world of Spillane and Bond crackles with fear, violence, and irrational behavior; society for them is filled with crime, evil, and guilt. Their job is to get those responsible, and it matters little if six or eight innocent bystanders become victims.

Millions of people read detective stories and each month other millions reach for *Playboy* or similar magazines. Even though these magazines aim at the twenty- and thirty-year age range, they unfortunately hit adolescents of all ages. To widen the appeal, these magazines now include a variety of material, ranging from interviews with the president to panel discussions on leisure and automation. Some of their offerings are contradictory to their basic point of view.

Their philosophy is most evident in their editorials, special display sections, and advertising, as they urge male readers to see themselves as happy-go-lucky, with women as playthings. They promote an attitude for boys in their late adolescent years of "eat, drink" and "make Mary," for life can be a lot of fun. This comes at a time when these boys react to hormonal changes with an increased awareness of girls.

This philosophy promotes a simplified view of life where "living life to the hilt" appears to mean a self-centered pursuit of the pleasures afforded by an affluent society—the "fashionable" in clothes, food and liquor, theater, books, music, and travel. Even more, "living life to the hilt" means the pursuit of sex as fun. This is life without commitment to anything more serious than providing conditions for one kind of gratification after another and with an understanding of life which is simplistic and shallow.

THE MEDIA

We are encouraged by the *Playboy*-like magazines to eat, drink, and seek the worldly pleasures of life, but television often portrays more violence than love. False and contradictory images are beamed into our homes, warping our values and promoting needless fears. Recent research has promoted an outcry that television violence is an environmental hazard and should be curbed. The U.S. Surgeon General, the American Medical Association, and the

P.T.A. have led the battle for a change in television's programming.

Dr. George Gerbner, professor of communication and dean of the Annenberg School of Communication of the University of Pennsylvania, has worked on this problem over the past ten years. He has recently revealed his methods of research, the results of his research, and the conclusions from the information collected. He defines violence as the physical force we experience when we are threatened with being injured or killed or are actually injured or killed.

Ten years of presidential commissioners, investigations, hearings, and information gathering has yielded damning evidence that television often serves us poorly. At this writing many network programs still contain violence. The overall rate of violent episodes is still large with children's cartoons averaging twice as many.

Violence on television is unlike that in movies or books for these reasons: we usually have television from the day we are born until the day we die, we usually don't have to leave home to see it, we don't have to know how to read, it is available to all classes and groups everywhere in the industrialized world, it is used nonselectively (people watch by the clock, not by the program, and the TV clock is on over six hours a day in the average U.S. household). TV is like the environment—it is everywhere and it is inescapable.

There is convincing evidence that television viewing does make an important contribution to the way people deal with reality. Heavy TV viewers (those persons viewing more than four hours per day), are more fearful, anxious, and mistrustful than those viewing less than two hours per day. Television violence, then, generates fear of victimization and a sense of insecurity as well as the readiness by some to take advantage of the fears of others. Children growing up with television learn its lessons and rehearse its roles. There is a whole range of consequences, more far-reaching than was originally thought, including the shaping of distorted conceptions of ourselves and our fellowman. The contribution of television to an occasional violent outburst is bad enough but the circulation of fear and rigidity among many is more damaging in its long-range effects. Our chief instrument for teaching relationships among people and cultural outlooks serves us poorly.

Our minds are bombarded continuously by mass media, books, magazines, newspapers, television, radio, music, and movies. These are a part of our world of assumption by which we gauge other people's actions, attitudes, and motives. This is also a part of our picture of ourselves, for our self-image reflects our judgment of how others think of us. These are some of the influences which create a different personality malfunction. We have an inadequate understanding of how personality develops and our treatment is consequently imperfect.

THE PERSONALITY PROBLEM

Thoughtful, experienced physicians take each patient's psychological makeup into account in evaluating his symptoms, in choosing his treatment, and in deciding what and how to tell him about his disease. Concepts of personality have been unclear in medical thinking for many years and the passage of time brings new explanations, but none totally clear.

Before the rebirth of clinical medicine in the seventeenth and eighteenth centuries, physicians characterized a patient's personality on the basis of his horoscope and not his behavior. Today this is regarded as nonsense. In the seventeenth and eighteenth centuries, most physicians discarded interpretations of astrology but continued to interpret personality in terms of the four "humors" of Galen. Patients, therefore, had a lymphatic, a sanguine, a choleric, or a melancholic personality. It was believed that the type of personality not only controlled the symptoms but also determined which diseases would or would not develop in different people. A great amount of medical writing, which considered this problem before the nineteenth century, is today regarded as unsound. The most useful concept of personality development for use by medical practitioners is the reaction-pattern concept. There is no doubt that how we react or think of ourselves determines in part the diseases we develop. Hence, we may relate the so-called psychosomatic diseases to abnormalities of the ego. If the ego structure or concept of self is weak—a "woe is me" attitude—there is likely to be more sickness in that person; his personality structure is inadequate.

Our personality comprises a central core of consciousness surrounded by all the interrelationships which we experience with family, friends, acquaintances, and strangers. In some persons this network of relationships is poorly developed, whereas in others we see a level of maturity indicating that the personality is highly developed. Development of personality is a search for relationships that makes us more personally and socially desirable. It gives us an outgoing personality. It enriches not only our own lives but society of which we are a part. This kind of self-seeking allows us to express our individual traits without injury or offence to our friends, family and acquaintances who share our everyday lives. On the other hand, if we have a detached personality which doesn't like closeness and relationships to other people, self-seeking means self-gain, rather than the more desirable self-seeking for development of the personality. Thus, when we assemble voluntarily in a social way, we serve a wholesome and desirable end. This is in contrast to the tendency to push children and also adults into groups, without regard to their choice in the matter. This creates more irritation than tendency to function together because it is not initiated by self-seeking and does nothing to nourish the personality.

CONSCIOUSNESS

If consciousness is the core of the personality, we can consider our own consciousness and its contents. It is a mixture of thoughts, fantasies, ideas, and sensations of the external world which we have seen, heard, and smelled. Objects appear, such as trees, cars, houses, and books. We are aware of people, as bodies in space, as personalities and voices. We spend a good part of our time moving about, actively regulating many things. We may turn the page of a book, drive a car, speak to someone, listen to a lecture. Normally our personal consciousness unfolds a picture of our surroundings for the primary purpose of helping us survive. Our consciousness is limited because it must busy itself selecting survival-related information from all the enormous variety of physical energies that we contact at each moment of our lives.

The atmosphere delivers energy in many forms: the electromagnetic fields, light, X rays, radio waves, and infrared radiation. In addition, there is mechanical vibration of the air containing sound waves, gravitational pull, atmospheric pressure on the body and gaseous matter in the air. Then we have our own internal drives or stimuli, thoughts, muscle activity, pains, feelings, funny feelings, and much more. These processes occur at the same time and continue as long as we live; yet, we are not aware of each process at each moment. Our personal consciousness, then, cannot fully picture the eternal or internal world but is only a small fraction of the whole "reality." Ultraviolet radiation, radio waves, and other forms of energy will be unknown to use for our eyes and ears have no way of detecting them.

Our consciousness is designed to warn us of the dangers which threaten us. It keeps its alertness through our eyes and ears and makes us ready to act when alarmed. In an earlier period when the danger of death or injury from animals or other humans was a part of daily living, man learned to select those sounds or sights which meant danger and from these a stable consciousness was constructed.

If then, our ordinary consciousness is something we must construct in order to survive in the world, there are several ways to construct it. And if our consciousness is a personal construction, then, we can change our consciousness simply by emphasizing one part of life over another. The process has been compared by the psychologist William James to that of a sculptor carving a statue out of marble. The process involves many levels of selection and consequent limitation, yet each individual sculptor's statue is unique, as is each person's consciousness.

We interact with the external world, select, and construct a personal world in several ways at the same time. We see things or hear sounds and the brain sorts and modifies them. This filtered information is compared with memory of the past and our expectations of the future, until, finally, our consciousness, constructed as a "best guess" becomes the cornerstone of our world of assumptions. This process offers stability but much of the information is useless and is discarded.

FURTHER CHARACTERISTICS OF CONSCIOUSNESS

Our consciousness is not altogether stable. We are each subject to moment-to-moment changes in our personal world. We each have a different past and background (schooling, jobs, special interests, etc.,) that in part make up our consciousness. Additionally, all of us, who live in a particular area, speak the same language, shop the same stores, and attend the same schools because of these common shared parts of life.

Our tendencies and assumptions don't stay the same, they shift, as do our needs and intentions. We are sometimes hungry, sometimes satisfied, sometimes tired, sometimes alert. Our consciousness is made different by the occasion and circumstance. When hungry, we seem to notice food smells and restaurants more than when we have just eaten. A plate of food looks far different if we are hungry than it does when we are well fed and content.

Our consciousness flows as a stream from one idea, object, or image to another. We maintain and refresh it through our thoughts. Our stream of thought is, more than any other factor, the foundation of normal consciousness. Since our consciousness is the core of our personalities and it normally is constructed from our stream of thoughts, then we may change our personalities by constructing a different consciousness through changing our stream of thoughts. We may go through life without suspecting the existence of potential forms of consciousness which may determine different attitudes, furnish a different formula and give a new image to a life of a different dimension. On the other hand, we could change our stream of thoughts to a higher level through study of the biblical teachings and philosophy's wisdom and through Christian thinking in obedience to the teachings of Christ.

EDUCATION'S ROLE IN BEHAVIOR AND PERSONALITY

Human behavior has been a puzzle for centuries with one theory after another. Educators have stressed the environment's role in shaping human behavior. Yet some philosophers disagree on the environment's role for it denies the role of human nature. Colleges and universities, emphasizing environmental forces, have changed their curricula away from a broad and general cultivation of the mind with its liberal doses of philosophy and literature. This has kept our thought patterns on a lower plane.

Why do we need to learn more philosophy? Why not teach more

HUMAN NATURE—WORRIED SICK

science or mathematics? Philosophy is knowledge just as mathematics, history, and science are knowledge. But philosophy differs from the other three in the way it asks questions. The philosopher appeals to the common experience of mankind.

Philosophical questions are among the most important questions we can ask. Philosophy asks questions about the world, as does science. But philosophy asks questions about what is right and wrong, good and bad. We live in a world in which scientific knowledge and technology have yielded the secrets of nuclear power over which we have less and less control. Philosophy asks questions about resolving differences between nations and individuals without resorting to the use of all the power we've developed.

Aristotle taught about the good life and the good society in concepts which are useful today. He thought of it in terms of living well. Living well means more than having wealth or health and more than having physical comforts and sensual pleasure.

For Aristotle, the basic goods that are ingredients in a good life were knowledge, wisdom, friendship, and love, and above all else, moral virtue. The most extraordinary thing about Aristotle's theory of the moral virtues is his point about their inseparability.

A person can't be courageous unless he's just; he can't be just unless he's temperate; and he can't be temperate, just, or courageous unless he's prudent. The four cardinal virtues are inseparable. Unless you have all four, you have none.

We make a poor choice when we select television, detective stories, or *Playboy* as a teacher of behavior, rather than philosophy. The weakness of our concentration bears witness to this poor choice. Go on a hiking trip with a typical American and listen to what he talks about. It will give a measure of the emptiness of his mind. He'll talk about food, weather, football, money, sex, and cars. He may seem to be having a good time but he lacks much that is needed for a genuinely good life.

In the course of our lifetime, under the influence of advertising, friends and acquaintances, we acquire and develop individual desires or "wants." These "wants" appear to be "good" because we want them.

In contrast to our acquired wants, we have certain natural needs.

We need food, clothing, shelter, sleep, knowledge, love, honor, respect. These natural desires or needs are common to all persons. They are built into our human nature. We face difficulty today in separating our needs from our wants. If we give in to our wants, buying more than we can afford, we suffer the attendant financial burdens and worries. The things we want may be good but only if they don't interfere with what is really good for us.

Philosophy is a teacher of the wisdom of life, helping us to listen, observe, measure, and calculate. It helps us to learn the difference between achieving happiness by fulfilling our needs and feeling happy which may be associated with what we regard as "good times." We learn that the stimulation we need, to avoid boredom, is well acquired by seeking knowledge rather than seeking things.

The emphasis of education recently shifted from the intellectual to the economic with a seeming atrophy of language and a paucity of knowledge of great literature. This has its consequences in personality building. Language was formerly considered a means of communicating information and ideas. Among many of the young it no longer is. For many young persons, and some of their teachers, in what used to be called English Composition, language is intended neither to transmit information nor display knowledge. Their way of talking has for such persons the main purpose of announcing to the world in general, but not to any hearer in particular, their habitually trivial feelings. The replacement of generally used speech by stereotyped phrases is an aspect of teenage behavior that puzzles and annoys those who love to speak well.

It is sad when a person of such limited language ability is unable to accommodate himself to variations in his intellectual environment. His language leaves him unable to adequately talk with persons from different walks of life or intellectual levels and leaves him incapable of developing or modifying his behavior in response to changing needs.

PERSONALITY DYSFUNCTION

Personality development is complex, subject to many influences and variations. These differences make life interesting as we meet and know different people. Failure of the personality to develop in a

HUMAN NATURE—WORRIED SICK **45**

mature way, or regression of personality may give rise to anxieties and antisocial behavior, with multiple symptoms from all body systems. Persons who experience these problems visit the doctor, have multiple laboratory and X-ray examinations with normal results, and serve as a source of considerable frustration. The doctor is frustrated because he fails to find a disease to treat. His therapy for the patient's problem is inadequate. Tranquilizers, referral to a psychiatrist, psychologist, or counselor may follow. The patient is frustrated because his suffering is unrelieved.

For the past several centuries, the causes of disturbed behavior have been the subject of widespread discussion, and today the focus is on adolescent and teenage peculiarities, for many of those with the problem are young people. Society, viewed as adverse and restrictive, was given the blame for years. This view was followed by the "age of alibis," resulting from the swing to permissive upbringing. Rejecting or domineering mothers were said to be responsible for all but a small proportion of abnormal behavior. The serious psychological stresses resulting from boredom, due to a loss of creativeness in our work, has been largely neglected by modern psychologists and psychiatrists. The worst factor may well be the crowding of people into cities and adjacent suburbs, as a result of the technological revolution; the effects of people on people.

SEEKING HELP AND BEING DISAPPOINTED

Millions of patients, with personality construction less than adequate, go to doctors for help. Solutions to this type problems are usually less than satisfactory. Doctors have paid far more attention to abnormalities of the body than to how those abnormalities are influenced by our thinking. Doctors are taught by other doctors and over the past seventy-five years, a model of medical explanation and treatment has developed with its own set of values and ways of solving problems.

Patients, on the other hand, have generally found this point of view inadequate. Much of the criticism of modern medicine is directed at the tendency to emphasize the changes in the body's fluids and functions, at the expense of the feelings, thoughts and fears of the patient.

Our personalities may lose their deep harmony, the doctor is interested in patching up our bodies, and our real need is to repair the alienation from God. Does a relationship to God build a sounder personality and remove the stumbling blocks which prevent healthier minds and bodies? In everyday life, doctors have the responsibility of observing and evaluating symptoms which arise from sickness and disease. Some symptoms will be the result of behavior disorders complicated by the use of drugs and/or intoxicants. Medical problems may be related to cigarette smoking, overeating, or lack of exercise. We fall short in our solutions to these problems.

But the doctor should be aware of the presence, the absence, and the strength of alienation from God in his evaluation of sickness. Spiritual values are intertwined with the network of cultural patterns and are a part of our interpretation and perception of sickness. Our relationship to the Creator adds a new strength in our search for motivation in changing bad habits. Patients often hesitate to disclose this vital part of their lives to doctors. We doctors should be more specific in our questioning in order to show patients that their values and ideas are of genuine interest and importance in the management of their problems. When we talk with patients, we often neglect to ask such questions as: What do you think has caused your problem? Why do you think your problem started when it did? What do you think this sickness does to you? How does it work? How severe is your sickness? Do you think it will last a short or long time? What kind of treatment do you think would be helpful for your sickness? What are the most important results you hope to receive from this treatment? What are the chief problems your sickness has caused you? What do you fear most about your sickness?

When we look at the effects of illness in a patient, we find one of four possibilities: it may threaten him; it may cause a loss of a part of his body or a loss of part of his body's function; it will be of no consequence; it will cause him to gain in a physical, mental, or spiritual way.

Before the unknown of an illness becomes known, there are periods of anxiousness, hopelessness, despair, worry, and there is a seeking, in some cases a desperate searching, for the doctor or doctors to solve the puzzle.

THE PLACE OF THE EMOTIONS

Emotional responses to the challenges of life may erupt in different forms: changing moods, erratic feelings, intense reactions. The type of emotional response, derived from a combination of causes, includes the type of nervous system we inherit from our parents, and the relationships and experiences which have formed our consciousness. Uncontrolled and conflicting emotions are a part of daily life for the great majority of us. One of the results of the fall from fellowship with God is that we do not experience an unconscious natural harmony between our understanding, our wills, and our feelings. The alienation of sin means that we are alienated not only from God and each other but also from ourselves.

The alienation of sin can play havoc in our understanding, our feeling, our choosing, and our responses. Our emotions are destructive for two important reasons. They are that part of us that is easily manipulated by outside influences; fad, fashion, or fancy. Once manipulated they become powerful persuaders; we may move in the wrong direction for some or all of life.

The emotions and the imagination may sometimes be under the control of understanding and reason but special conditions need to be met before they are effectively tamed. Conversion to belief in Jesus Christ is a complete change involving the whole person, it may be profoundly emotional. The emotions alone, however, do not affect conversion from a sinful life to a life of belief in Christ. Christianity, in fact, provides a basis for the highest place for the emotions, but in coming to believe and live like a Christian, the place for understanding, reason, and truth are primary and the place for the emotions is secondary.

The balance we seek between understanding and emotions is fine in theory but it is quite another thing to maintain that balance every day as we continue to believe. The control of the explosive power of the emotions in our lives is perhaps the single greatest human factor in explaining why faith does not continue as it began. Emotional balance is attained as we mature in the faith through study of the teachings of the Bible and through our prayerful communication with God.

4
Cancer—A Threat to Life

In the spring of 1958, my youngest brother, B. H., called to tell me that he had found a swollen gland in his neck. He did not feel sick, had lost no weight, had no pain, and was working daily. In eight months he was dead. The gland was swollen with abnormal cells, spread from a malignant focus in the testicle. The growth in the testicle was too small to detect. Frequent examinations would not have yielded an earlier diagnosis; he had no warning until the cancer had spread. In 1958, chemotherapeutic drugs were powerless in controlling this particular type of cancer.

CANCER—IS THE SOLUTION NEAR?

Cancer, a group of diseases, is found in all races and ages of man and in all other animal species. Doctors and laymen alike have often thought of cancer as a single disease. In a sense this is true; all cancer is characterized by unrestrained growth of cells. There are, however, great differences among various forms of cancer. A description of cancer (its location; severity; related causes, if known; tendency to spread to other sites, and progress) emphasizes the importance of considering it as a collection of diseases—skin cancer, lung cancer, leukemia, cancer of the bowel, and so forth. Growths, called tumors, are not all cancerous; some are benign. Not all cancers are fatal.

In 1900, tuberculosis was the leading cause of death in the United States, heart disease ranked fourth, cancer ranked eighth. Today cancer is the second most frequent cause of death. At present, the chance that a person now under twenty years of age will develop cancer at some time during his or her life is about one in four for males and slightly higher for females.

What are the chances of survival if you get cancer. This is not an easily answered question; it depends on many factors. Two of the most important are the site of the tumor and the extent of disease when treatment is started. Other factors include age, sex, race, general health of the patient, and the method of treatment.

Consider again the case of my brother—had he noted the enlarged gland today, he would probably have had a better chance of survival. It is true that during the intervening twenty-year period, even in the most difficult cases of cancer, some progress has been made. New drugs have been discovered, new information is available about nutrition and supportive care. Forty years ago, a patient with cancer had a 20 percent chance of living five years; today the figure is 33 percent, and continued improvement is expected in the decades to come. Each year 600,000 Americans are found to have cancer and the chance of eradicating it as a threat remains remote.

There are, however, three distinct approaches to the problem of cancer: early detection, improved treatment, and prevention. Much emphasis has been placed on early detection; informing physicians of diagnostic improvements, informing the public of danger signals, and alerting them to the need to seek professional help if their symptoms suggest cancer. It is with newer approaches to treatment and prevention that I intend to deal further.

IMPROVED TREATMENT

Removing the lymph node from my brother's neck today would be a far different process than was present in 1958. Fighting his cancer would mean more than excising the tumor and focusing the latest chemotherapy in the hope of killing all of the abnormal cells. (The mind exerts powerful effects on the body; these powerful forces, mind and body, must unite.) Failure to use these potential allies could mean the loss of the battle to the "enemy" through resistance to treatment, depression, and loss of will to live. Therapy, to be effective, must treat the healthy portion of the body and mind as well as combat the diseased cells.

B. H. would likely experience a sense of helpessness and depression. This is normal for cancer patients, a serious accident, the death of a loved one, a debilitating illness of any loss over which there is no control. Under usual circumstances with cancer, however, B. H. would find this helplessness magnified, for a number of reasons. (1) The belief that cancer is equivalent to death; (2) the feeling of being a victim and suffering; and (3) the vast complexity of the treatment planning and implementation, which tends to take all decisions about treatment out of his hands.

There is some evidence that feelings of helplessness and depression are involved in the cause of cancer. These feelings are likely to worsen under cancer treatment; B. H. may have felt that he had nothing to say about these treatments, that his actions were futile, that he had no control over his body.

A HEALTHY IMAGE—EVEN WHEN DISEASED

B. H. would have needed a mental image of his disease and his body, influencing the direction of the body toward health or disease. He could, conceivably, have defined his tumor as a "small, malignant tumor with spreading to the lymph nodes in his neck." He could have accepted the presence of some cancerous cells in part of his body while the rest of him was healthy.

This point has been stressed by Dr. O. C. Simonton as he describes the cancer cell as a "very weak, confused cell." He states that it only grows when bodies are weakened and that a normal, healthy body rejects and destroys cancer cells "thousands and thousands of times during a normal, healthy lifetime." In his care of patients with cancer, Dr. Simonton, in an audiotape, states that patients can more completely cooperate with their treatment by visualizing the radiation or chemotherapy entering the body and killing the cancer cells. Normal cells may be damaged, but they recover; the weak, confused cancer cells cannot repair themselves. B. H. could have visualized his white blood cells as soldiers attacking and destroying the cancer cells. Cancer grows, not because the body cannot destroy cancer but because the white cells stop attacking, as if there were a depression in the immune systems, not unlike the depression often found in the patient.

STRESS MANAGEMENT

It is impossible to know whether stress played a part in B. H.'s cancer occurring at this particular time. He was, at that time, attending college, working a full-time job, and caring for his wife and young daughter. Research has repeatedly shown that chronic or intense stress is involved in the body's production of hormones and the efficiency of its mechanisms to detect and destroy cancer cells. People are worried over many things, guilty over some things, and pressured from many sides with deadlines. If a loved one is lost, a change in job or location is advised, or an injury or sickness occurs, the body's immune system is overtaxed and the adrenal glands are in a state of chronic overuse. Patients can be taught to reduce their stress. Energy can be released to stimulate the defense against cancer cells and permit the adrenal glands to recuperate from their abused state.

Stress management teaches patients self-control over their pulse rate and other physiologic states using relaxation and biofeedback techniques, and control over external stresses, using assertiveness training. The patient needs a sense of effectiveness in gaining control over his life and in coping with this extremely stressful period in life.

PHYSICALLY DYING—SPIRITUALLY SOUND

My brother, B. H., had no fear of dying as death drew closer. I have no way of knowing how he felt earlier. Telling him that he had cancer was one of the most difficult tasks of my professional life; it was not made easier by coming during my first year of practice. He took the news in stride, prepared his will, withdrew from school but worked as long as he was able. During this period, he was visited by his pastor many times; benefitting from the pastor's comfort and counsel, and even to making his funeral plans.

B. H. had lived well; thus, he died well. He was at peace with God and his fellowman. He was a loyal, dedicated husband and father. He searched for and found the deeper meaning of life. His funeral, in accord with his wishes, was an expression of love for those he was leaving, cautioning them to so live that they would stay in a close relationship with God.

CANCER PREVENTION

The third approach to cancer is that of prevention which is the ultimate goal in the control of disease. In this case we are talking of avoiding the cause of cancer or protecting against the cause. Removing or avoiding those dangers that result in cancer is either an individual or public decision. From an individual point of view, the preventable cancers are those due to cigarettes, alcohol, and diet.

Information about the risk of cancer sometimes creates a reaction that is the opposite of what is intended. The World Health Organization widely circulated a recent publication in which it was estimated that 70-90 percent of all cancers are environmentally related. Dr. Michael J. Halberstam, editor of *Modern Medicine Magazine*, commented that the estimate is misleading and far from universally accepted in the scientific community. It leads to an air of fatalism expressed in a bumper sticker which says "Life Causes Cancer."

The estimate is misleading, says Halberstam, because a person tends to think of environmental factors as those substances in the air, food, and water over which he has no control. Cancer epidemiologists, however, are referring to everything but heredity. Thus, many of the environmental factors that the epidemiologists refer to are factors over which the individual has varying degrees of control. They include such proven or suspected "life-style" cancer-causing agents as cigarette smoking, drinking alcohol, excessive fat in the diet, excessive radiation from X rays, certain drugs and chemicals, and overexposure to sun.

ENVIRONMENTAL EXPOSURE

At a recent health conference in Washington, the experts agreed that only a relatively few of the 65,000 or so existing chemicals have been shown to cause cancer. About 300 of these have been shown to cause cancer in animals and only 26 of those are known to cause cancer in humans. It is estimated that only 2 to 3 percent of the chemicals tested in the future will prove to be cancer causing.

Cancer from exposure to chemicals was first described by Percival Pott in 1775 after he noted the occurrence of cancer of the scrotum among chimney sweeps. Lung cancer was found among miners exposed to uranium in 1897 and bladder cancer was discovered in Aniline-dye workers in 1895.

Occupational hazards are not limited to the workers in a particular plant, but extend over a more general area and population. Industrial fumes are difficult to contain. They pollute the air of wide expanses of land and water. In addition to these sources of chemical threat, our environment includes additives, preservative, flavoring, and colorings in our foods: perticides, herbicides, cosmetics, deodorants, paints, and drugs.

Such products are assayed for safety but the task is monumental. The Delaney Clause of the Food and Drug Act prohibits the use of cancer-producing chemicals in food in any amount. This law, sound in principle, is often opposed by the public and by the company manufacturing the chemical in question.

X RAYS AND DRUGS

Most of us are exposed to X ray for the diagnosis of an illness sometime in the space of a lifetime. X ray is an irreplaceable diagnostic tool in medicine and is paradoxical in that it both causes and cures cancer. Exposure to X rays is an acceptable risk when it is used to search out the cause of a symptom but unnecessary exposure is to be condemned. This is particularly true for pregnant patients to reduce the chance of exposure of an unborn baby.

The consequences of drugs also include effects on unborn babies. The most striking example is the development of cancer of the vagina in the daughters of mothers given the drug to assure the continuance of the pregnancy. The old adage "anything that can cure cancer can cause cancer" is relevant to drugs used in cancer chemotherapy, especially if these drugs are combined with X ray therapy. Patients with arrested cancer are in greater danger of developing a second cancer, probably through the effects of these cancer drugs on the body's mechanism to remove abnormal cells from the bloodstream.

CANCER AND OUR DIET

Researchers have already linked excessive use of salt to hypertension, excessive use of sugar to diabetes, and excessive fat from animal and dairy foods to heart disease. There is now a convincing correlation between the foods that Americans put on their tables and the most frightening of all diseases—cancer.

The link between diet and cancer has even become a political issue. In widely publicized hearings in July 1978, the Senate subcommittee on nutrition cited evidence that half of all cases of cancer are related to diet. Meanwhile, as if to underscore the subcommittee's questions, Dr. Barry Commoner of Washington University in Saint Louis reported that hamburgers fried in metal pans contain substances that cause changes in bacteria that could lead to cancer.

Actually, National Cancer Institute researchers have studied for years to clarify the relationship between foods and cancer—particularly cancer of the digestive tract, which alone accounts for 172,600 of the 600,000 new cases of malignant disease that occur in the US each year. They have also begun to suspect a link between fats that we eat and cancer of the breast, affecting annually about 90,000 women in the US. The precise link between diet and most cancers, however, is far from clear-cut. "Diet is not a cause per se," says Gio Gori, chief of the National Cancer Institute's Diet, Nutrition and Cancer Program, "but simply a factor that may potentiate or retard the functioning of other cancer promoting factors."

EATING HABITS

Americans, Scots, New Zealanders, Canadians, and Danes eat large amounts of beef which is rich in animal fat, and thus have more cancer of the bowel. The Japanese, whose traditional diet is low in fat, have less than a third the American incidence of bowel cancer. But Japanese-Americans, who have adopted the Western taste for beef and butter, run essentially the same bowel-cancer risk as other Americans. On the other hand, Seventh-Day Adventists, many of whom are vegetarians, have a lower rate of bowel cancer than do their countrymen as a whole.

Fiber-containing foods, especially fiber from grains, is thought to provide protection against bowel cancer by absorbing or diluting the irritating or carcinogenic materials in foods. The Finns, for instance, eat as much fat as the Danes, their neighbors, but they eat a great deal more fiber and they have a relatively low rate of bowel cancer.

HORMONE BALANCE AND DIET

The risk of breast cancer also varies with the fat content in the diet. Japanese women have one fifth the breast cancer rate of

American women. Japanese-American women, however, eating the usual American diet, have the same amount of breast cancer as their Caucasian counterparts. Dr. Ernest Wynder of the American Health Foundation suspects that fat affects balance of female hormones. One recent study of women has shown that switching from a high fat to a vegetarian diet lowers levels in the blood of prolactin, the hormone responsible for breast function. It remains to be proven, however, whether a change in eating habits will reduce breast cancer risk in women. Cancer of the endometrium (the lining of the uterus) and of the kidney has been associated with obesity in women. Eating less, particularly fewer sweets, would reduce weight and conceivably reduce the risk of these types of cancer.

PREVENTIVE ACTION

We have learned from the history of medicine that illnesses can be prevented even though the specific mechanism of cause is not understood. The same concept applies to nutrition and cancer. "The Prudent Diet" has been advocated as an approach to prevention of heart disease as well as other vascular diseases. Such a diet, because of its limitation of fat, should prove valuable in reducing the risk of cancer of the bowel, breast, endometrium (uterus), and kidney. The prudent diet suggests limiting the consumption of red meat to four portions per week, eating no more than two eggs a week, limiting the intake of high cholesterol foods, and avoiding fat-rich dairy products and saturated fats. We should eat more fish and poultry, egg substitutes, and replace whole milk with skim milk. We should increase the fiber content of our food, most easily done by using bran. We should increase our intake of Vitamin C; it neutralizes the effects of some cancer causing compounds. Dr. Linus Pauling suggests the use of two grams of Vitamin C daily to provide this effect.

IS YOUR JOB CAUSING CANCER?

No longer are accidental injuries and plant disasters the overriding concerns of workers in industry. The invisible contaminant, in the lead smelter, plastics factory, the synthetic rubber plant, or the hospital operating rooms, may initiate a change of events resulting in death or crippling disability twenty or so years after the initial exposure.

Our modern industrial age, born of the boom of postwar chemical knowledge, is now under scrutiny. Petroleum, petrochemicals, and automobiles have replaced steel and railroads as the backbones of the nation's economy. This era of "better living through chemistry" may well have exacted a hidden toll from all Americans.

Much of the story of the toll of workers in shipyards and other workers exposed to asbestos during World War II is now unfolding. Asbestos seems to be everywhere. Resistant to fire and virtually indestructible, it has been used in a wide range of products from brake linings to wallboards. Exposure levels have already been reduced due to improved workplace conditions but those workers with exposure years ago, especially if they also smoke cigarettes, stand a risk of lung cancer that is ten times that of the general population.

The asbestos experience as well as many others has accelerated the deadline for cleaning up the workplace. Every day at least one new chemical is added to the environment. Americans are more aware now than ever that occupational disease involves more than the worker. As former HEW Secretary, Joseph Califano, told an AFL-CIO Conference on Occupational Safety and Health: "We have learned, often by tragic experiences, that Kepone, undetected in the workplace today, flows insidiously into our streams and rivers tomorrow, that occupational exposure to asbestos today is tomorrow's exposure of our families at home and our children in school. . . . By protecting workers today, we are likely to make the greatest gains in our efforts to protect the rest of society."

PROSPECTUS

The dream of cancer research is to add cancer to the diseases that can be truly prevented and controlled, by measures that would retire surgery and radiation as the primary forms of treatment. The obvious progress being made in research, particularly in the fields of virology and immunology and in the arena of molecular biology, augurs that the goals may be achievable. Until then, however, much can be done by the full application of what is known and available.

Primary preventive measures are essentially based on two considerations: (1) the removal or reduction of causative agents from contact with the susceptible population and (2) the protection of the members of the population against exposure to causative agents. Both approaches need exploitation for the most effective results. The availability of immunization procedures against waterborne bacterial diseases does not allow reduced attention to clean water supplies; both are necessary. In the same manner, future discovery of a viral entity that might be involved in the initiation of lung cancer in no way reduces the problems of air pollution or of tobacco smoking. Exposure to carcinogenic agents usually presents problems other than cancer, because neoplasia is but one of many end points of chronic toxicity and irriation.

Cancer is a large group of diseases and not one entity. The approaches to causation, prevention, detection, and treatment must be different for different forms of cancer. The causes of many cancers are quite clear such as the tobacco-genic cancer of the lung. Avoiding cancer where the specific cause is known may necessitate the change of a habit or the change of a job to avoid the chronic exposure of the irritating substances.

Within the framework of general prevention, it remains important to eliminate skin lesions, plaques, and scars, to maintain good oral and dental hygiene, to repair chronically inflamed areas, and to retain a high index of suspicion when confronted with the many danger symptoms that could connote cancer. Suggested changes in eating patterns are rational and easily made. The full value of this change will take years to prove.

5
Human Nature — Seeking Healing

There is hardly a man living, be his disease what it may, who will bear to believe himself beyond the possibility of restoration to health. He will allow the physician to profess palliation and postponement, and relief; and, when the physician does all which he professed to do, he will be thankful to him, but he will think it strange that he can do no more. And so he lets go his faith and his allegiance, and goes in search of some one to cure him by a lucky remedy.

Thus, the comparison of what we can do with what we are expected to do, is often mortifying enough. But it cannot be helped. People are free to expect what they like; while we cannot do more than can be done. Our ability is bounded by the nature of things, at all events.

> Dr. Peter Mere Latham
> Lectures on Clinical Medicine, 1836

God works by means, as Christ cured the blind man with clay and spittle. As we must pray for health of body and mind, so we must use our utmost endeavors to preserve and continue it. Some kind of devils are not cast out but by fasting and prayer, and both necessarily required, not one without the other. For all the physick we can use, art, excellent industry, is to no purpose without calling on God: it is vain to seek for help, run, ride, except God bless us. Hippocrates, an heathen, required this in a good practitioner, and so did Galen.

> Burton
> Anatomy of Melancholy, 1561

Modern medicine has made miraculous discoveries, but there are areas where it is not nearly as effective as people believe it to be. Some people think that medicine is misdirected, representing a poor investment by the public. If medicine is misdirected, a false assumption about health lies at its base. This assumption has largely been unquestioned until recently and centers about the concept of the body as a machine that can be protected or rescued from disease by chemical and physical intervention. Medical teaching, rooted in seventeenth-century science, took this direction, but was indifferent to the influence of the primary cause of poor health/personal behavior.

Doctors, hospital staffs, and medical schools are searching for the main influences on health with emphasis on personal behavior. The public, on the other hand, is having to reorient its thinking, for it still considers the early discovery of disease and proper treatment by the doctor to be the primary route to health. The public's idea should be modified to recognize that many diseases cannot be cured, and that a healthy body is largely the result of our way of life. It is one thing to hear someone tell us of the influence of tobacco, alcohol, drugs, unrestricted eating, and slothful living on our health; however, the decision to give up a habit or change a life-style is not easy. Effective ways have not been found to convince millions of people that they should eat differently, be more active, give up cigarettes, alcohol, and drugs, or counter the stresses of life by a healthier reaction to these stresses.

PREVENTION—A MYTH?

Consider medical efforts in prevention of several diseases over the past fifteen years. Though it had been suspected long before 1964, the Surgeon General in that year reported the inescapable causative effects of smoking on lung cancer, heart disease, and emphysema. Following this, cigarette advertising was banned on television and radio and warnings were placed on cigarette packages. Smoking is now being banned in public places. The evils of smoking have been taught in our public schools for the past twelve years. What has been the effect? There is no wave of rejection of cigarettes. Young people, particularly young women, are smoking more than ever and the tobacco industry flourishes.

Venereal disease, another of the diseases receiving major attention over the past fifteen years, has become a national epidemic. In

1977, there were one million reported cases of gonorrhea. (The teaching of VD prevention falls on deaf ears.) Family planning, contraceptive advice and materials are readily available, yet illegitimate births are common and socially acceptable. Meanwhile, abortion, an emotional controversy, seems to be far from a solution.

Alcoholism, a problem as old as mankind, is increasingly present in our families. Drug use and abuse waxes and wanes, depending more on the availability of drugs and the vigilance of law enforcement than on the efforts of doctors. In the more stable population groups, taking prescription drugs for tension relief is the norm. Some people have difficulty coping without tranquilizers.

A generation of school children taught to know the four nutritious food groups, flock to fast-food chains where fat, salt, and sugar—the most abused basic insults to our diets—are served in extravagant abundance. Sugary cereals, candies, and sweet snacks, accentuated by poor dental hygiene make dental caries almost universal. Obesity is a national health disgrace, as is the lack of exercise. We would rather ride than walk.

The leading cause of death among young adults is not a disease; it is automobile accidents. Drivers pay little attention to the 55 miles per hour speed limit, which did help reduce highway deaths. Compulsory seat belt laws died a natural dealth. The motorcycle helmet requirement is regarded by some as an invasion of privacy. Alcohol abuse and driving make a lethal combination, particularly during holiday periods, although only slightly more so than on any weekend from midnight to 4 AM. Healthy lives are often shortened or disabled because of diseases and automobile accidents.

The factors that affect our longevity and health are heredity, environment, and life-style. There is little one can do about the first, a little more the second, and an inadequate disposition to do much about the third. These three feed upon each other; to these add frustration, boredom, anger, alcohol, tranquilizers, brutality and we have now an endless stream of people who are making visits to doctors for their physical health and mental health and to psychiatrists or psychologists for their emotional disruptions. The cost of these visits is staggering.

There has been very little information accumulated, documenting either the cost benefit or cost effectiveness of devoting more resources to personal preventive medicine. Yet, each "new" health plan rediscovers prevention. We could put a clinic or a physician's office on every street corner and it wouldn't make any decisive change. Some people would rather be sick than well; would rather be sick than sacrifice anything. They are disposing of their health carelessly. For many people, a visit to the doctor may be a satisfying experience. For a short while, someone listens to troubles and appears to care. The physician may sympathize, cajole, or chide, but at least the patient is reassured by the doctor's presence. The patient leaves, perhaps with a transient desire to improve or mend his wicked ways, but he probably won't change his life-style.

MODIFYING BEHAVIOR: DOES IT WORK?

People have always been thoughtless and shortsighted in regard to their health, but recognizing human fraility is no excuse. In spite of this, man has emerged the winner in centuries of competition with other animals of the earth. We have acquired ranges of behavior of a unique and extraordinary complexity. Language, one of our greatest achievements, has led to the social environments which have produced art, literature, religion, law, and science. Difficult problems have been solved with the technologies of physics and biology. Yet, with respect to our own behavior, something always seems to go wrong. In medicine, the question is asked: "When shall we have the behavioral science technology we need to solve patients' problems?"

The more appropriate question is: "Will people change if we teach them what to do?" Physicians, teaching mothers in Kenya to boil water and feed their children eggs instead of cassava (a root with little food value), will often be discouraged because mothers prefer doing things in their old way. They may do it this new way for a while, but soon it becomes too much trouble or the old habit is simply too strong.

Human behavior is complex. We may be able to explain why we do or don't do certain things but solutions are not easy to impose on unwilling people. People are said to act as they do because of their feelings, their state of mind, their intentions, purposes, and plans.

They act because they will to act. Changing human nature is not easy.

PSYCHIATRY: A FADED HOPE?

Critics, both within and outside of the medical profession are questioning both the effectiveness of psychiatry in treating neuroses and abnormal behavior, and the evidence that allegedly proves that psychiatry heals. Seven million patients spend $2 billion each year in search of psychic perfection, or, at least, relief from the pain of living. Some of these would vote that psychotherapy does work; others would vote that it does not work. The argument within the profession becomes heated over whether psychotherapy is a science or a superstition evolved into a discipline. The majority of psychiatrists still practice under the guidance of Freudian principles as their model, but for the past twenty years an increasing number are sharply challenging the need for long-drawn-out analytical sessions struggling through childhood events at $20 to $100 per hour.

Martin Gross, in his recent book *The Psychological Society,* has analyzed the impact of psychiatric therapy beginning with Sigmund Freud. At the time of Freud's visit to the United States in 1909, psychology was in its infancy. Today, psychology is regarded variously as an art, science, therapy, religion, moral code, life-style, philosophy, and cult. As the Protestant ethic has weakened in Western society, we can see a new psychologically directed man in operation. Instead of seeking rules and life cues from outside sources, he pays for hints from experts who tell him what to make of himself and others, how to live and even how to feel.

The quest for psychotherapy is part of modern man's search for the elusive goal of normality. The boundary between the well and the sick has been blurred by psychology and psychiatry. "Now every normal person is only approximately normal," Freud reminded us shortly before his death. "His ego resembles that of the psychiatrist in one point or another, in a greater or lesser degree." This idea labels us all, to some extent, as being sick. We have falsely equated mental health with the unusually unreachable ideal state which combines success, love, and lack of anxiety. We are thus all sick, for normality is almost unattainable, according to Freud. What psychiatry and psychology have done is to redefine normality. The pain reactions to the normal problems of life, despair, anger, frustration, loneliness, guilt have been labeled as abnormal behavior.

Gross points out that researchers are saying that psychotherapy is not a science or even a technology with a predictable outcome. It is a personal encounter between two people, a healer, and a patient. Naturally, something has to take place during the patient's visit. The discipline of psychotherapy is not the healing agent. The more obvious explanation is the substitution of psychotherapy as a key ritual of a psychological religion. If the therapist is believable and the patient has faith, there follows a series of explanations providing the reason for the emotional disturbance. These psychological explanations may be nonsense, but they provide a placebo effect and set the stage for a long-term and intimate relationship which provides the real potential for healing. Is it possible that some of the views of psychology, including psychotherapy, are a disguise for a new spirituality, with each of the types of therapy having a different faith? Could it be that faith itself, not the doctrine, is the healing agent?

If faith heals, how is it accomplished? Gross believes that psychotherapy and primitive faith healing operate by a similar mechanism. It is suggestion; the skill of directing a patient or believer, without his knowing it. A superior patient is psychologically minded, reasonably intelligent, anxious, verbal, and not very sick. Success in therapy is to some measure determined by the same factors that help make for success if life. It has been found in one research study to be simply the result of whether the therapist and patient found each other likeable and attractive.

Gross concludes that this new psychological society is substituting for the loss and dilution of formal religion and seeking a creditable base that would be as reputable in the last half of the twentieth century as Christianity was in the first. Psychology and psychiatry in assuming that special role offer mass belief, promise of a better future, opportunity for confession, unseen mystical workings, and a trained priesthood of helping professionals devoted to servicing the participants, of whom there seems a never ending stream. In filling the void left by Christianity, psychotherapy has created images that parallel older spiritual ones. The therapist becomes a godlike figure, dispensing wisdom ot those who come with their troubled lives.

HOLISTIC HEALTH

A growing number of people have emphasized the failures of modern medicine. Their disillusionment arises partially from unrealistic expectations. Perfect results have been expected from the doctor, but life is not that sure or that simple. Patients may not get better, the surgery may not be successful, complications may arise. Part of the problem comes from our tendency to endow new advances of medical science with promises of cures that are not delivered as time passes. New drugs and miraculous breakthroughs paint a rosey picture but often the patient feels no better after the treatment and his health is unimproved.

Many patients are changing in attitude from a passive, uninvolved relationship to an active, responsible role in regard to their state of health. Care of their health is no longer in the same category as taking the car to the garage for a tune-up or repairs. They are asking questions and new methods have been sought.

This search has brought converts to "holistic health" (often called wholistic). The term is derived from the Greek word *holos* meaning "whole" in the sense of "entire" or "unified." This movement emphasizes unorthodox approaches to the healing of sickness. The patient is offered "wholeness" through a bewildering array of possible treatments; acupuncture, psychic diagnosis, vegetarian diets, and core energetic therapy to list a few of many.

The impersonal nature of much traditional or institutional medical care, such as big hospitals, causes resentment in people. They feel as though they are composed of organ systems being poked and prodded by multiple specialists during a major illness. Patients have a real and legitimate need to be treated as people. The holistic movement recognizes this, but most good physicians recognize this, also. The element of personal concern and attention is particularly missed by patients who are in a large teaching hospital.

A patient comes to the doctor expecting to feel better after the treatment but the nature of his problem is not clear. He may be tired, his energy is gone. The doctor can't locate the cause. He does laboratory tests, X rays, and so forth, in search of something to cure; he finds nothing. The patient is still tired; but now he's soured on doctors and resents the expense of his tests. He might feel reassured by the pronouncement that nothing abnormal has been found, but not always. These criticisms of medicine's shortcomings should be a springboard for an objective inquiry, to consider the questions being raised and to look for answers. The holistic approach seems to be designed to provide an opening for a preconceived answer, rather than to encourage discussion in an open, objective fashion.

Holistic medicine criticizes other modern medical care in an unbalanced and unfair fashion. Responsible criticism should be based on a recognition of the legitimate accomplishments of doctoring, of which there are many. The message, to be read between the lines of criticism in the face of the achievements of medicine, is that medical success does not completely resolve or solve the human condition. In order to deal with the root of the problem of humanness, a religious answer is needed, and the holistic movement provides that, in a manner similar to many of the Eastern religions.

Unfortunately, a big problem with the answer provided by holistic medicine is the lack of essential honesty and truthfulness. It's the same with any of the occult or esoteric approaches to spirituality. There is a basic spiritual pride involved in the assumption that the ignorant masses can be conned into enlightment, while pretending to do something more trivial, such as relaxing them or making them successful in business or healing their ailments.

In holistic medicine, the religious answer is packaged in a way that leads you to think it is really just medical treatment or technique which will be helpful, even though a bit strange. Once begun and accepted, however, you will be led step by step into the full-blown religious solution—unless you recognize its meaning and resist at some point. The religious solution, in this case, has great similarity to transcendental meditation.

CHRISTIAN HEALING: A REALITY?

The grass-roots revolt against the sterility and arrogance of the world view promoted by materialistic science has been paralled in

Christian circles by a rising interest in divine healing. Some Christian groups, notably the Pentecostal churches, have long sustained a tradition based in part on claims of supernatural healing. Now, however, even denominations which lack such a tradition are developing an interest in it. It may well be that the concerns and developments that have brought "holistic healing" into the secular limelight have also produced a fascination with the possibilities of divine healing within the church. In any case, questions about healing are being asked by Christians, and church leaders are having to rethink many of their traditional views on the subject. Hardly any theologians would make Christian healing a cardinal doctrine of the Christian faith.

We hear the terms "divine healing, supernatural healing, miraculous healing," and "Christian healing." John Stott states that "all healing is divine healing, whether without the use of means or through the use of physical, psychological, or surgical means." Many physicians feel that this observation is valid in its context but prefer to restrict the term "divine healing" to cases in which God intervenes directly, bypassing the natural processes of the body and the skills of doctors and nurses. "Supernatural healing" is generally thought of as equivalent in meaning to "divine healing" while "miraculous healing" is reserved for cases of supernatural healing that are unquestionably beyond the range of normal possibilities. "Christian healing" refers specifically to healings that occur through the agency of a Christian intermediary; a human representative of Christ who functions as a "healer."

One deceptively simple question raises uncertainty and dispute: Does divine healing occur today as it did in New Testament times? The question requires consideration of multiple factors. Four of these come from the Bible: (1) the works of Jesus and his teaching concerning them, as described in the Gospels; (2) the healings performed by the disciples and apostles, as described in the Gospels and the Book of Acts; (3) the references to healing, as well as the references to sickness, in the Epistles; and (4) the specific instructions for healing given by James. The other two factors are more difficult to evaluate, no matter if you strongly believe them or disbelieve them. These are the cases of extraordinary cure that are contrary to what is expected from a medical viewpoint; and a consideration of those cures that have either resulted from suggestion or are not cures at all, only a mometary relief of symptoms. In addition, we must consider, as well, the fact that many patients experience no change, despite the most fervent prayer and healing efforts.

HEALING IN THE BIBLE

1. JESUS AS HEALER

Healing experiences account for almost one fifth of the entire Gospels, exceeded only by the emphasis given to miracles in general. Jesus used varied methods in healing. In most cases, He both touched and spoke to those seeking healing (Peter's mother-in-law, Luke 4:38-39 and the two blind men, Matt. 9:27-30). When healing the lame man beside the pool of Bethesda (John 5:2-9), Jesus only spoke to him. Occasionally Jesus used a physical medium; for example, the mud and saliva for the blind man (John 9:1-7). He healed the centurion's servant from a distance (Matt. 8:5-13). The woman who touched the hem of Jesus' robe (Mark 5:25-34) and the crowds (Matt. 14:36) were seemingly healed without Jesus' intention being involved. There is at least one case of "gradual healing" (Mark 8:22-25) in which the blind man first perceived "men as trees, walking" and then had his sight restored completely.

There is no recorded occasion on which Jesus made an attempt to heal that resulted either in failure or in an incomplete healing, although Mark 6:1-5 reports that the unbelief of those in his hometown prevented his working any miracles there; even so, "He laid his hands upon a few sick people and healed them."

2. HEALING PERFORMED BY THE DISCIPLES AND APOSTLES

The "sending of the twelve" marked the beginning of the disciple's healing career. "And he called to him his twelve disciples and gave them authority over unclean spirits, to cast them out, and to heal every disease and every infirmity" (Matt. 10:1, RSV).

Mark 6:13 records the disciples' success without giving details. In the Book of Acts, various Christians performed healing but in many of these cases almost no details are given. In two cases involving Peter and Paul, healings occurred virtually without the exercise of an intent from the healers. In Acts 19:12 it is reported that cloth which had touched Paul was used as an instrument of healing.

In one instance, the disciples botched the healing of a child with an evil spirit. The anxious father came to Jesus after first consulting the disciples unsuccessfully. The case was undoubtedly difficult, but Jesus cited the lack of faith and the need of prayer and fasting for a successful conclusion (Matt. 17:21; Mark 9:29).

3. HEALING AND SICKNESS IN THE EPISTLES

Though there are four listings of gifts in the Epistles, the gift of healing is mentioned in only two of them (1 Cor. 12:8-10,28-29). The same epistle refers to sickness caused by ungodliness, specifically in regard to irreverence toward the communion supper.

Elsewhere, however, it is merely mentioned in passing that Trophimus was sick (2 Tim. 4:20). Reference to Paul's "thorn in the flesh" is not clear, though it has been mentioned that it was a physical ailment (2 Cor. 12:7). It is also argued that Hebrews 12, which deals with a Christian response to suffering, refers to endurance when sickness is sent by God.

4. HEALING INSTRUCTIONS

Specific instructions for healing are given only in James 5:14-16. "Is any among you sick? Let him call for the elders of the church, and let them pray over him; anointing him with oil in the name of the Lord; and the prayer of faith will save the sick man, and the Lord will raise him up; and if he has committed sins, he will be forgiven. Therefore, confess your sins to one another, and pray for one another, that you may be healed. The prayer of a righteous man has great power in its effects" (RSV).

In the light of the reference to gifts of healing in the Epistles, it is interesting that James did not mention people with the specific ability to heal, but delegated the healing responsibility to the elders of the church. It should also be noted that oil was one of the most common substances used for medicinal purposes in the ancient world.

EXPERIENCE AND OBSERVATION

It is one thing to believe that divine healing occurred frequently during Jesus' day and in the days of the early church, but quite another to say that it is, or should be happening today. If the Christians who claim to be involved in divine healing are correct, then we should be able to find documented cases where divine healing occurred which is unexplainable by the normal standards of medical care. As a matter of fact, such cases should be fairly frequent, if divine healing is God's general will. On the other hand, if claims are made in ignorance or in error, then every case of claimed healing should be explainable by some principle known to modern medical science. Unfortunately, it is not that simple. The medical profession knows very little of the effect of the mind upon the health of the body, and it is this area that is chiefly involved.

If one of the body's organs or systems fails to function or functions improperly, and has no damage to its structure, it is a functional illness. Skipping or palpitations of the heart, for example, are often the result of tension, stress, fatigue, or excessive stimulation from coffee and tea. Yet, there is no damage to the wall of the heart. The heartbeat is not under voluntary control, yielding instead to the influence of the autonomic nervous system. Organic diseases, on the other hand, involve damage or change in the structure of an organ or system. Gallstones, infection, cancer, or a heart attack are all organic diseases. Functional, but not organic, ailments can sometimes be influenced by suggestion; particularly if the persuader has a forceful personality and is likely to evoke significant faith from the patient. So, if certain of a patient's symptoms are from a functional problem, it is practically impossible to demonstrate that cure was not the effect of the suggestion.

Another significant difficulty is the proof that cure has occurred. In order for a claimed case of healing to stand up to skepticism, it is necessary to have access to the patient's medical records and to have a sound understanding of the nature of the disease and of the change that is claimed to have taken place. In addition, other possible causes of the cure must be eliminated.

Attempts to clearly research this question have been intriguing, but not conclusive in either direction. Highly respected Christian physicians have cared for patients whose recovery is regarded only as due to the direct intervention of God. Father Francis MacNutt cites several cases in his description of Christian healing *(Healing, and the Power to Heal)*. Reports such as these reflect careful judgments, but the experience of a few people cannot by itself prove to a skeptic that divine healing is or should be, a normal activity of modern Christianity. On the other side, Dr. William Nolen, in his book, *Healing: A Doctor in Search of a Miracle,* gives an interesting and well-researched account of "miraculous healing," claims which he concluded to be false. These claims were all taken from patients attending meetings of the late Kathryn Kuhlman. It would be too simple, however, to make a statement that God is not actively healing people in extraordinary ways based on the fact that not one person was healed at a particular place or time.

CONCLUSIONS

It is an evident fact that if divine healing is occurring today, it is not going on in quite the same way it was in the days of the early church. Many of those sick today are sick of chronic diseases; they recover slowly, if at all. The success rate of Jesus was 100 percent, and the recorded experiences of the disciples indicate a very high rate of successful cures. These cures were usually instantaneous, and even "slow" cases recovered within a few hours. Is it not reasonable to ask why, if God is in fact actively, divinely healing today, so many people are not healed? Father MacNutt, from his experiences in healing services, gives eleven reasons why healing may not be occurring in a specific case.

(1) Lack of faith, *specifically that of the healer.*
(2) God is using the sickness for a purpose.
(3) The patient attaches a false value to suffering and doesn't want to get well.
(4) "If there is a sin connected with the physical ailment, . . . no healing is likely to take place unless the sin is dealt with first."
(5) Not praying specifically—especially in cases of inner healing, where God may use some of the "natural processes of psychological healing which requires that incidents which have been . . . hidden in the subconscious be brought to conscious light and these be healed by Him."

(6) Faulty diagnosis and praying for the wrong kind of healing; for example, praying for physical healing where deliverance or inner healing is needed.

(7) Refusal to see medicine as a way God heals.

(8) Not using the natural means of preserving healing—ignoring the body's need for rest or not correcting an imbalance in life-styles.

(9) Now is not the time (some are healed instantaneously, some have delayed or gradual healing, and others are not healed).

(10) A different person is to be the instrument of healing.

(11) The social environment prevents healing from taking place—that is, the ailment is the result of a problem in our relationship with other people and will not be cured until that problem is solved. Thus, the healer's first requirement is for discernment as to when to pray, for whom to pray, and how to pray for healing.

In the final analysis, the differences between the present time and the era of the early church are conditioned by the historical circumstance of the two times, the trials of the church in each, and the purposes of God in relation to each of these. There are different strengths and weaknesses between the early and modern churches. The early church functioned under the immediate threat of persecution. The Book of Acts emphasizes the feeling of "community" as believers. Problems were handled by getting together and praying. Their healings were instantaneous and clearly miraculous. We, in contrast, live comparatively quiet lives; the concept of Christianity is recognized, if not understood, by much of society. Our problems are usually personal, and we tend to deal with them on our own. Perhaps God's healing in a divine way is only after concerted, long-term prayer commitment by a group of Christians, not because he needs more prayer hours than he did 2,000 years ago, but because he thinks we need to spend more time together in prayer.

6
An Assessment

To be what we are and to become what we are capable of becoming, is the only end to life. —Spinoza

INTRODUCTION TO CREATIVITY

To change an existing situation is often a major undertaking. It demands creative behavior to find the clear path out of a dilemma. It is necessary to become aware first of the situation that needs improving; second of the essential components of the problem; and third of the skills and methods required to manipulate that problem condition into a better state.

Changing behavior demands creativity. It is not a cold analysis of the facts or needs and then recommending a major overhaul. Creative solutions lead, inspire, and provoke. They are the beginning to a more advanced development of differences in our behavior and consciousness.

Creativity can be defined as both the art and the science of thinking, reasoning, and behaving with both subjectivity and objectivity. This combines our feelings with our knowledge. When we become more creative, we become awake to our feelings and our knowledge. This forms a "creative" wholeness which allows us to see ourselves in a different way. We determine our goals, design the reason for going, and lead out; on the way to success with its joy of accomplishment.

ANALYZING YOUR LIFE-STYLE
INTRODUCTION TO ANALYSIS

The thought of analyzing a life-style, or of analyzing any situation can appear to be a boring and dry (but necessary) step along the way to an exciting solution to the situation. Analysis is an equally exciting step if we understand it as the state when most of our learning takes place. Failure to understand the problem is a major cause of failure in overcoming an unhealthy life-style. How else can you reveal your existing knowledge about your life-style, rearrange this knowledge in orderly fashion, and then relate new knowledge to it, other than through an analysis of your life-style? The process of analysis shows the many interrelationships between the various parts of a life-style.

The Basic Questions

Questioning your life-style calls for courage. It means throwing off fear and pride as you determine what, who, where, when, and why.

The questionnaire that follows is designed to help you estimate the status of your health. There are four divisions: personal habits, mental health, fitness, and spiritual health.

Wellness Appraisal Section

Instructions: You are experiencing a certain level of wellness. Determine that level by answering these questions. If you are unsure of the answer to a particular question, leave it blank, and go to the next one.

1. Eating is one of the joys of my life.................... True   False
2. I do not salt foods without thinking or tasting .... True   False
3. I eat a good breakfast............................... True   False
4. Fresh fruits and vegetables, cooked and uncooked, are a part of my daily diet................................ True   False
5. I understand the importance of fiber in my diet and know its sources .... True   False
6. I am careful to restrict the use of sugars and other refined foods in my diet .... True   False
7. During breaks at work I regularly get coffee, a soft drink, or a pastry from the vending area .... True   False
8. I usually drink three to four glasses of water daily .... True   False
9. For lunch I usually eat a steak or hamburger .... True   False
10. My largest meal is in the evening .... True   False
11. I usually sit and watch television after eating the evening meal .... True   False

12. My diet is balanced and doesn't require supplements .... True False
13. I do a self-breast or self-testis examination every month .... True False
14. Each year my doctor examines my breasts .... True False
15. I have a pap smear every year .... True False
16. I smoke cigarettes every day .... True False
17. I drink some alcohol every week .... True False
18. I brush and floss my teeth every day .... True False

Mental Health

1. I enjoy life .... True False
2. I enjoy going to work .... True False
3. I feel that my judgment is sound .... True False
4. When I make a mistake, I am able to admit the mistake and learn from it .... True False
5. I react with anger when my point of view is rejected .... True False
6. I can usually say no without feeling guilty .... True False
7. I set limits for myself and stick to them .... True False
8. I regard my opinions as valuable, but I respect the opinions of others .... True False
9. I usually solve a problem through the way I feel about it rather than through what I know about it .... True False
10. I find it easy to laugh .... True False
11. I enjoy my family.................................... True False
12. I am able to give and receive love .... True False
13. I make and maintain friendships easily .... True False
14. I accept the responsibility for my actions .... True False
15. I feel my job is ethically within my personal/spiritual values .... True False
16. I usually have plenty of energy........................ True False
17. I usually meet my need to sleep .... True False
18. I am able to relax my body and mind without drugs .... True False
19. I recognize and meet my sexual needs within my personal/spiritual values .... True False
20. I have no money problems .... True False
21. I can clearly differentiate between my needs and my wants ... True False
22. I set goals and priorities for myself and my family .... True False

Fitness

1. My pulse rate, at rest, is 60 beats per minute or less .... True False
2. I have learned how to count my pulse .... True False
3. I usually take stairs, rather than ride elevators or escalators .... True False

AN ASSESSMENT

4. I run, bike, or swim for at least one hour a day three or more times a week .... True False
5. I play a strenuous sport, such as handball or racquetball, three or more times a week .... True False
6. I walk briskly two or more miles a day................... True False
7. I run or jog at least one mile four times a week .... True False
8. I run or jog at least one mile two times a week............. True False
9. I have a sedentary job, such as desk work................ True False
10. My daily activities involve vigorous physical effort (such as construction work, farming, moving heavy furniture, etc.)....................................... True False
11. My daily activities involve modest physical effort (such as gardening, rearing young children, cleaning house, etc.)... True False
12. I experience shortness of breath if I walk up a flight of stairs .... True False
13. When I carry as little as twenty pounds for one city block on level surface, I get very tired .... True False
14. The fat and skin of my arms measures more than one inch by the "pinch test." (Pinch the skin and fat of the back of the upper arm between the thumb and index finger, remove the measuring fingers, maintaining the space represented by the fat layer. If it measures over one inch, the fat layer is too thick) .... True False

Spiritual Assessment

1. I regularly read the Bible .... True False
2. I believe the main theme of the Bible is Jesus Christ .... True False
3. I believe that the Bible is God's word to man .... True False
4. I believe that, if I meet the conditions stated in the Bible, its promises will be fulfilled in my life..................... True False
5. I believe in God the Father, the Son, and the Holy Spirit..... True False
6. I believe that God reveals himself as the Being to whom we are accountable for our moral acts .... True False
7. I believe that God has revealed himself through his design of the universe .... True False
8. I believe that God is holy .... True False
9. I believe that God is just.............................. True False
10. I believe that God is love .... True False
11. I believe that Jesus is God's Son........................ True False
12. I believe that Jesus died for my sins .... True False
13. I believe that I must confess my sins daily to remain in fellowship with God.................................. True False
14. I hate my brother, yet I claim fellowship with God .... True False

15. I can't stand my neighbor, yet I claim fellowship with God . . . . True False
16. I don't get along with my spouse, yet I claim fellowship
    with God . . . . True False
17. I never attend church, yet I claim fellowship with God . . . . True False
18. I am satisfied with my relationship with God . . . . True False
19. I live each day exalting God . . . . True False
20. I choose God above money . . . . True False
21. I choose God above personal ambition . . . . True False
22. I choose God above self . . . . True False
23. I choose God above human love . . . . True False
24. I believe the secret of effective living in the Holy Spirit . . . . True False
25. I regularly pray unto God the Father . . . . True False
26. I pray in the name of Jesus . . . . True False
27. I believe the secret of effective prayer is praying in
    the Holy Spirit . . . . True False
28. I pray according to the will of God . . . . True False
29. As I pray to know the will of God, I am prepared to submit
    to it . . . . True False

Cancer Self-Questionnaire

Patient Questionnaires, evolved over the past thirty years, have been used to alert physicians to a point of interest in the patient's history, or to a symptom suggesting the need for further examination. These questions are derived from the questionnaire used by The Strong Clinic in New York City. Their complete questionnaire, ten pages in length, was developed to discover thirty-one diseases in the early stage, seventeen of which are forms of cancer.

Urinary Tract   **No Yes**
1. Has a member of your family ever had cancer of the kidney
   or bladder?   ___ ___
2. Have you ever had a urinary tract infection?   ___ ___
3. Have you ever had blood in the urine?   ___ ___
4. Have you ever had kidney stones?   ___ ___
5. Have you ever had any chronic kidney disease?   ___ ___
6. Do you work close to cleaning fluids, paints, dyes, or
   benzidines?   ___ ___
7. Do you have a more frequent urge to urinate?   ___ ___
   With the passage of small amounts of urine?   ___ ___
   Primarily during the night?   ___ ___
8. Do you have pain or burning on urination?   ___ ___

AN ASSESSMENT

Male Reproductive   **No   Yes**

9. Has a member of your family ever had cancer of the prostate or testicles? ___ ___
10. Have you ever had mumps? ___ ___
11. Have you ever had an undescended testicle? ___ ___
12. Have you ever had inflammation or enlargement of the prostate gland? ___ ___
13. Do you have persistent pain or discomfort in the testicles? ___ ___
14. Do you have swelling of either testicle? ___ ___
15. Do you have difficulty in starting the urine stream? ___ ___
16. Do you have swelling of either breast? ___ ___

Female Reproductive

17. Has a member of your family ever had cancer of the cervix, vagina, womb, or ovary? ___ ___
18. Have you ever had a miscarriage? ___ ___
19. Have you ever had an abnormal "Pap" smear? ___ ___
20. Have you ever had an ovarian tumor or cyst? ___ ___
21. Have you ever had a fibroid tumor of the uterus? ___ ___
22. Have you ever had a polyp of the uterus or cervix? ___ ___
23. Do you have irregular menstrual periods? ___ ___
24. Do you have vaginal bleeding between menstrual periods? ___ ___
25. Do you have persistent vaginal discharge unrelated to menstrual periods? ___ ___
26. Do you have vaginal bleeding after sexual intercourse? ___ ___
27. If you have gone through the menopause, do you have any bleeding or spotting? ___ ___
28. Do you use birth control pills? ___ ___
29. Do you use female hormones (estrogens)? ___ ___

Breast

30. Has a member of your family ever had cancer of the breast? ___ ___
31. Have you ever had cysts of the breast? ___ ___
32. Have you ever had a tumor of the breast? ___ ___
33. Do you have breast pain related to your menstrual cycle? ___ ___
34. Do you have breast pain not related to your menstrual cycle? ___ ___
35. Do you have a lump in either breast? ___ ___
36. Do you have a change in the usual shape of the breast? ___ ___
37. Do you have any discharge from the nipples? ___ ___
38. Do you have any ulceration; eczema or scaling of the nipples? ___ ___

Skin and Lymph Nodes

39. Has a member of your family ever had cancer of the skin? ___ ___

	No	Yes
40. Has a member of your family ever had cancer of the lymph nodes?		
41. Have you ever had cancer of the skin?		
42. Have you ever had a mole removed?		
43. Have you ever had a skin tumor removed?		
44. Have you ever had X-ray treatment of the skin?		
45. Have you ever had a burn with scarring?		
46. Do you have unexplained, generalized, persistent itching?		
47. Do you have unexplained sweating during the night?		
48. Do you have repeated episodes of unexplained fever?		
49. Do you have swelling or enlargement of glands?		
50. Do you have persistent, nonhealing ulcers or sores?		
51. Do you have patches of skin with persistent eczema?		
52. Do you have any moles which have changed color, changed size, become ulcerated, or bled?		

Neuromuscular and Skeletal

53. Do you have persistent or recurrent headaches?		
54. Do you have any fainting episodes?		
55. Do you have recurrent arthritis?		
56. Do you have weakness of either arms or legs?		

Lungs

57. Do you have a chronic cough?		
58. Have you coughed up blood?		
59. Does mild exertion cause shortness of breath?		
60. Do you smoke cigarettes?		
61. Is your strength becoming less?		
62. Are you losing weight without dieting?		

Gastrointestinal

63. Have you vomited blood?		
64. Have you passed blood from the rectum?		
65. Have your bowel movements been darker than usual?		
66. Is your appetite poorer than usual?		
67. Do you have persistent, recurrent nausea?		
68. Do you have recurrent abdominal pain?		

7
A Healthier Heart

The road to a healthier heart through exercise is paved with good intentions. If you doubt it, look in your own closet: jogging shoes, tennis rackets, bicycles, and weights, purchased because of advertising's lure or a fleeting desire to "get into shape" are now stuffed into distant corners—to avoid the feeling of guilt every time the closet door is opened. The same evidence could be found collecting dust in millions of closets, attics, and garages.

Millions of Americans, however, have joined the "fitness renaissance" in deadly seriousness—turning to jogging, running, calisthenics, tennis, swimming, and weight lifting in quest of better health. Most of them are interested in the $64,000 question. Does regular, vigorous exercise really give protection against heart attacks? Some believe it without knowing the facts, and they recruit others with evangelistic fervor. The answer, according to a study presented at the American Heart Association's last meeting, is a resounding yes! Dr. Ralph S. Paffenbarger, Jr., based these conclusions on his records of 17,000 men, age thirty-five to seventy-four. Dr. Paffenbarger believes that it's the total amount of energy expended that counts. As the level of activity increased in these men, the incidence of heart attack decreased. Two thousand calories of effort a week seemed to be a crucial figure. Those spending less than this in exercise were 64 percent more likely to suffer heart attacks than those who spent more. This group of men had 572 heart attacks. Dr. Paffenbarger estimates that 166 of these would never have happened if they had exercised at the 2,000 calories level or higher.

Many people are chained to their desks daily by their jobs—these findings are of especial importance to them. Earlier studies had found that men with physically demanding jobs, such as longshoremen, had fewer deaths from heart disease than those who did sedentary work. These studies suggest that those with desk jobs can gain the same advantages by physical activities during their leisure time.

A study in England confirms this finding. Three hundred thirty-seven working men, most of whom had jobs of light activity such as bank clerks and bus drivers, had their diets and heart disease rate analyzed for ten years. Surprisingly, those who ate the most had fewer heart attacks; the physicians studying the problem reasoned that, since their weight remained constant, the big eaters must also be the big exercisers. It was so; the high-calorie men were much more active in their leisure time than those who ate less. Dr. Paffenbarger's study concludes that this protection against heart attacks is still effective regardless of other factors which might increase the risk of heart attacks (cigarette smoking, high blood pressure, or a family history of heart disease).

Changes are produced by exercise which lead to a high level of protection from heart attacks. These facts we know: (1) heart rate and blood pressure are lowered—thus, less oxygen is needed; (2) fat levels in the blood are lowered; (3) carbohydrates are burned more efficiently; (4) less adrenalin is pumped when we become excited; (5) blood is less likely to clot, reducing the chance of a clot forming at a "plaque" in the coronary arteries. It may be that exercise enlarges our coronary arteries, permitting greater blood flow or develops new blood channels, but neither of these is proven.

We can't wait around expecting new facts to give us total knowledge before acting. Life isn't like that. We are not able to have total knowledge about anything. What we need is wisdom. We have given in to the easy life during our leisuretime. It is far better to live lean than to rest complacently on our broad derrierés with an attitude of "having it made."

NEW SPRING IN THE STEP

Essentially the heart is the organ that needs additional strength to withstand life's stress, but the legs and other muscles become stronger in our efforts to make the heart stronger. What can we hope to gain for all this effort? In the first place, the benefits are predictable—it is not a gamble. Secondly, the long walk, hiking over mountain trails, the touch football game, or working in the yard are enjoyed for a longer period without dropping from exhaustion. Thirdly, the heart and blood pressure behave economically—they respond more easily when sudden emotional or physical demands are made upon them. Fourthly, dispositions are improved, digestion is better, sleep is sounder, and the challenges of life are conquered with new spirit.

Being strong and being fit may not be the same. Lifting weights brings strength to the arms of a weight lifter, but he must train his heart to improve endurance and to get a "good wind."

BETTER LOOKING THROUGH EXERCISING

Reuben painted ladies with well-rounded arms, legs, and bodies in the Renaissance age but that's not the look of today. The healthy, trim, vivacious look is gained through a combination of exercise and diet. Exercise alone is only moderately successful in weight loss. After all, it takes twenty minutes of walking to burn the calories in one apple. More strenuous effort, such as bicycling one hour daily, five days a week for one year, will cause a weight loss of twenty-five pounds provided the food intake doesn't increase during that time.

The most realistic and ideal combination is exercise with a prudent diet so that the loss in pounds is actually a loss of obesity. Exercise primarily changes body composition—fat into muscle. Young men are about 12 percent fat and young women about 25 percent fat with obvious body differences. These percentages increase as we age. Much of the remaining weight is made up of muscle, bone, blood, and other tissues, all combined under the term "lean body mass." We can see then the difference between being overweight and being obese. An athlete may weigh more than he should but still have only 12 percent fat—he is overweight but not obese. Obesity may overtake him if he quits playing ball and quits exercising but continues to eat as much as usual. Exercise training helps achieve a normal balance between lean body mass and fat but adding diet control means a loss of flab and a trim, firm, healthy figure.

BEGINNING—SAFELY AND GRADUALLY

Sometimes the determination and enthusiasm to begin an exercise program is tempered later with regrets. It is not just the aching muscles and joints—these are predictable and will ease—but one serious chest-pain episode will dampen the enthusiasm of the whole neighborhood. Hidden or silent heart disease may be present in 10 percent of the men over age thirty-five but in only 1 percent of men less than thirty-five according to the American Heart Association. Even so, with proper precautions and stepwise progression most of these will be able to exercise without harm.

There is no way to be sure that a sedentary male, age thirty-five or older, will escape a heart episode, but a physician's checkup is recommended and will give some reassurance. This should include a check of the heart, lungs, blood pressure, muscles, joints, an EKG, blood cholesterol, triglycerides, and hemoglobin. An exercise stress test adds additional knowledge. It is a very safe, moderately reliable indicator of the likelihood of silent heart disease and predicts the level of activity safely attainable. The information is then used to set both the limits of the exercise program and the rapidity of its advancement.

Are these tests absolutely necessary before beginning? The answer is no. Circumstances and common sense guide us in this. If you are forty or younger, fairly active without symptoms, and the tests are not easily obtained or are too expensive—you might forego them. The blood tests are more reasonable, more easily obtained, and could represent an adequate choice without having the stress test done.

On the other hand, if you have had a problem with your heart, even if apparently recovered, a physician should be consulted before beginning a potentially vigorous program. The medical questionnaire which follows will help guide you in making the decision.

A note of caution: It is risky to jump into an activity requiring a sudden burst of strenuous effort if your body is unprepared. A high level of exercise is to be achieved gradually and once achieved should be maintained. Long layoff with sudden intense exercise is to be avoided. This is worse than no activity at all.

MEDICAL QUESTIONNAIRE

If you answer yes to any of these questions, consult the doctor before beginning an exercise program.
I. Known or Unknown Heart Disease
   A. Have you ever been told by a doctor that you have heart trouble?
   B. Do you have a history of rheumatic fever, rheumatic heart disease, Saint Vitus' Dance, or absence from school as a child for painful joints?
   C. Has a heart murmur been heard when the doctor examined you?
   D. Have you been suspected of having or have you actually had a heart attack—under the following names: coronary occlusion, myocardial infarction, coronary attack, coronary insufficiency, or coronary thrombosis?
   E. Do you have chest pain or tightness on exertion, after eating, when walking in cold weather, or when upset?
   F. Have you ever had an abnormal electrocardiogram—either at rest or while exercising?
   G. Does your heart beat fast or irregular at times?
   H. Have you ever taken digitalis, quinidine, or any other heart medication?
   I. Have you ever used nitroglycerine, oftentimes labeled TNG or NTG, under the tongue for relief of chest pain?
II. Heart Attack Risk Factors
   A. Have you ever had diabetes, high blood sugar, or sugar in the urine?
   B. Have you ever had high blood pressure or hypertension?
   C. Has your blood cholesterol been high enough for the doctor to recommend a diet or medications to lower it?
   D. Do you weigh twenty pounds more than you should?
   E. Did your father, mother, brother, or sister have a heart attack before age sixty?
   F. Do you smoke more than a pack of cigarettes per day?
III. Other Limiting Conditions
   A. Do you have any chronic illness?
   B. Do you have an abnormal lung condition such as asthma or emphysema?
   C. Do activities make you short of breath that don't bother other people in a similar way?
   D. Do your legs cramp if you walk fast for one to two blocks?
   E. Do you have a high uric acid, gout, or arthritis?
   F. Do your muscles and joints move easily or are they likely to be aggravated by exercise?

THE HEART—THE PULSE—THE LUNGS

As normal active people exercise, the heart beats faster and breathing becomes more rapid—more oxygen is needed by the muscles to produce energy. All of the body's cells must have oxygen, nourishment, and a method of waste removal. The heart, operating like a muscular double pump, pushes 8,000 gallons of blood through 12,000 miles of blood vessels every twenty-four hours. Red blood cells carry the oxygen in their hemoglobin, releasing it to the cells and picking up waste products. At this point of exchange, the blood loses its bright red color, becomes dark bluish-red, and switches out of the arteries, into the veins.

The kidneys, acting like a giant filtration plant, take most of the waste from the blood. The carbon dioxide which remains is breathed into the air through the lungs. As we breathe in, oxygen in the red blood cells is replenished and the blood becomes bright red again.

The heart can't beat a normal 70-80 beats per minute at rest and then respond to a sudden 100-yard dash by increasing to 500 beats per minute. Neither can the lungs respond by increasing breathing from 14 breaths per minute to 70 breaths per minute during the same 100-yard dash. Both have limits beyond which they cannot go.

We can handle a small oxygen debt when our effort is greater than the ability of our hearts and lungs to supply oxygen. For example, the 100-yard dash is run as fast as we can but at the finish line we have to stop. Our legs have built up an oxygen debt but they are now at rest. The heart continues to race and breathing is still hard—the oxygen debt is being paid. To continue running at the same speed would lead to collapse if we did not take time to pay the debt.

While exercising, particularly early in the program, you need to know just how fast the heart is beating. It's impractical to count the heartbeat by holding the hand over the heart. It's more easily done by counting the pulse at the carotid artery, on either side of the neck just below the angle of the jaw or at the front of the wrist, near the base of the thumb. Count your pulse for 15 seconds and multiply by four to get the number of beats per minute. Counting the pulse within 15 seconds of stopping an exercise activity can do two things: (1) indicate your level of physical fitness; and (2) set a pulse target

A HEALTHIER HEART

zone which indicates that your effort is truly strenuous enough to strengthen your heart and lungs.

Before beginning a program, you can test yourself by walking up the stairs of an office building—five and one-half flights in three minutes or by fast walking—just short of running—for one-half mile in six minutes. Compare with the following results within fifteen seconds after stopping:

Pulse Rate	Condition
140 or more	poor
130	fair
120	good
110	very good
110 or less	excellent

In the second place, the pulse tells us if we are in the target zone as we exercise. (See the following table.) Too much exertion can be harmful but too little exertion will not do the job of strengthening the heart, lungs, legs, and arms. Our resting pulse can only increase to a certain point, depending on age, so exercising hard enough to push it beyond that point is dangerous. From a practical standpoint, we try to reach a "target zone" of 70-80 percent of our maximum rate. To exercise below 70 percent of our maximum pulse is of little benefit and to reach above the 85 percent adds very little for all the extra effort. The following table lists the target zone for different ages.

Age	25 Yrs.	30 Yrs.	35 Yrs.	40 Yrs.	45 Yrs.	50 Yrs.	55 Yrs.	60 Yrs.
Target zone (85%)	170	165	160	155	150	145	140	135
70-85% of (70%) Maximum pulse rate	140	135	130	125	120	115	110	105

AIMING AT THE TARGET ZONE

The heart can't develop into a more efficient pump by aiming at the target zone and missing. It is crucial that the pulse rate stay within the zone for 20-30 minutes. Seventy percent of the maximum pulse will do fine for conditioning the heart but if a more vigorous workout is desired, the 85 percent level provides the upper limit. It is wise to stretch with calisthenics for about five minutes before exercising to avoid sudden taxing of the heart. In addition, the joints and muscles are more supple with less danger of injury.

After exercising vigorously, you should coast at a reduced pace to allow the heart a gradual return to a resting level. Sudden stopping may trap blood in the muscles, slowing blood flow to the brain and heart with dizziness or faintness as a result.

FITNESS? WHAT KIND AND HOW MUCH EXERTION?

Your aim is to strengthen the heart, lungs, and circulation. They must be challenged. All activities do not offer the same challenge and some are not useful in achieving the aim of a healthier heart. Heart muscle, as well as arms, legs, chest, and so forth, are strengthened by increasing their flow of blood. This fact emphasizes the basic difference between isometric and isotonic or dynamic activities. Isometrics, such as weight lifting causes muscles to contract, squeezing arteries and reducing blood flow. By way of contrast, we see a runner with a churning motion of his arms and legs. This at first tenses and then relaxes muscles, pushing blood along the artery—much as the heart does when it pumps the blood—his blood flow is increased.

Isometrics will improve an athlete's skills at the same time it makes his muscles firmer and stronger. On the other hand, running, swimming, and other similar dynamic activities improve endurance, through strengthening the heart, lungs, and circulation. A program using both isometric and dynamic activities (combining weight training with a running program) will achieve both aims—firmer muscles and a stronger heart. This type of combination raises us to a higher level physically and mentally with new confidence in our bodies and with less fear of being overcome by the crises of life. We are better able to cope with physical and mental stress. Our thinking is clearer, minor normal symptoms are ignored, the doctor sees less of us. However, we still have to know what type of activity will raise us to this level.

ENERGY—HOW MUCH IT TAKES TO WORK AND PLAY

Everybody doesn't use the same amount of energy in doing the same thing; some are more skilled; some must rest more often; others will be bothered by the weather, etc. These factors make the use of a table which compares energy output less than perfect, but it

A HEALTHIER HEART

still shows us how many calories a certain activity will burn. For example, shoveling dirt, ten pounds per shovelful, at a steady pace for 10 minutes burn 70-80 calories, or 7-8 calories per minute.

	Activity		Calories/Hr.	Time needed to burn 2000 Calories
Poor	Desk work Driving auto Typing	Standing Walking 1 mi/hr Playing cards	120-150	15 hours
Minimal	Auto repair Radio-TV repair	Level walking 2 mi/hr Bowling, Golf with cart, Wood working, Playing piano, Horseback riding (walking), Skeet, Shuffle- board, Riding lawnmower, Bicycling 5 mi/hr (level surface)	150-240	10 hours— may be useful for those with low capacity due to age or medical problems
Good	Digging garden Shoveling loose earth	Walking 4 mi/hr, Bicycling 10 mi/hr, Ice or roller skating, Canoeing 4 mi/hr, Horseback riding (Posting to trot)	360-420	5 hours
Better	Digging ditches Carrying 80 lbs. load, Sawing hardwood, Shove- ling 10 lbs. for 10 minutes.	Walking 5 mi/hr, Bicycling 12 mi/hr, Tennis (Single), Water skiing, Jogging 5 mi/hr, Basketball, Mountain climbing, Squash, Touch football, Swimming (crawl 45-yd./ minute)	500-660	3½ hours
Best	Shoveling 16 lbs.	Cross country skiing 5 mi/hr, Karate, Running 7 mi/hr, Competitive handball, Racquetball or Squash.	700-800	2.6 hours

MAKING PROGRESS

Not much time has to pass before you begin reaping the benefits from your efforts. After two weeks or so you will have to work a little harder to reach the target zone, and your resting pulse is slower. The heart has already improved its efficiency. Sleep becomes sounder and end of the day tiredness is less. You begin to feel such an invigorating feeling that you hate to skip a day of exercise. Then, instead of finding excuses for missing a session, your frame of mind improves to a positive note where you work around interruptions in order to skip something other than the exercise.

Becoming "trained" makes it easier to work at the same level but you have to aim at a new level for further progress. For example, brisk walking has raised your pulse to the 70 percent level of your target zone after three to four weeks, but you are less tired and click off the distance with less effort. Then, start to jog for part of the walking time, checking your pulse as directed. When jogging becomes too light, try running. If you ride a bicycle, try a different route with more hills. As you progress, put a little more effort into your action.

THE RATING OF DIFFERENT SPORTS IN PROMOTING PHYSICAL FITNESS

JOGGING AND RUNNING

Jogging and running are usually regarded as the most efficient and inexpensive approach to improving endurance. Muscles will not be enlarged beyond their natural size. Running faster and faster is of no great advantage. The same calories are consumed in a mile run that takes eight minutes as in a sixteen-minute mile. The pace and distance can fit individual conditions and even those who had medical problems or are older can start slowly and advance to a higher level. It squeezes a maximum consistent effort into a minimum amount of time.

BICYCLING

Bicycling is another excellent activity to promote endurance if done regularly at a good pace. It can be done alone—so it doesn't have to be programmed into other people's schedules. It develops legs and back muscles but the seat of the bicycle must be adjusted so that the leg is fully extended when the pedal is closest to the road.

SWIMMING

Swimming is an excellent all-around activity which is good for total body conditioning. It is nonweight bearing and people with hip, knee, or ankle problems can still swim. The muscles that act against

A HEALTHIER HEART

gravity are neglected and an ideal balance would be to alternate swimming and jogging. Its only drawback is that a pool is required.

ICE OR ROLLER SKATING

Few adults indulge in skating activities unless they learned them as children. These sports are excellent for endurance and strengthen the pelvis and legs but for ideal all-around development should be supplemented with upper body exercise.

HANDBALL/SQUASH/RACQUETBALL

When vigorously played, fast ball games like these will provide a maximum of exercise in a minimum of time. The stimulation of endurance is excellent. Should warm up before playing. They promote coordination and agility.

ALPINE SKIING—DOWNHILL AND SLALOM
NORDIC SKIING—CROSS COUNTRY AND JUMPING

Both forms of skiing provide excellent fitness but there is a need to be in good condition to avoid injury. Nordic skiing burns more calories and promotes better endurance. Both are expensive and require equipment, and usually, travel time.

BASKETBALL

Basketball is a sport for those already fit. It will maintain endurance if played regularly but requires the assembling of several other people into a team. Injury to ligaments and strain on joints discourages many in the post-collegiate years.

TENNIS

Tennis is a great game to keep you fit if you run for the balls. It makes people anxious if they worry about their game. It is a moderate endurance exercise but this depends on how you play the game. Doubles will be slower and not require as much energy.

CALISTHENICS

A good calisthenic program should contain relaxing and limbering of exercise, should build up slowly from relaxation to warm-up to workout and then to cool-off and finally relaxation. Flexibility will be improved, but endurance depends upon the vigor with which it is pursued. If vigorously done, muscles become stronger and endurance is promoted.

WALKING

Walking is excellent for "reconditioning" but will not do much for those in "good" condition. You must walk fast and have enough time to walk a good distance. The biggest advantage is that anyone can do it, alone, in pairs, in groups, and so forth. It is moderate exercise for endurance.

GOLF

Golf is a fine recreational pastime which does little or nothing for fitness unless you walk and carry your clubs on a hilly course. Even then the "fretting" generated by your "game" might offset the benefit by disturbing your digestion and sleep.

SOFTBALL

Softball is excellent recreation but provides little exercise—too much time sitting around doing nothing.

BOWLING

Bowling is another pleasant recreation which is not particularly useful in promoting fitness but is better than nothing.

VOLLEYBALL

Volleyball demands less than basketball and teams are easier to organize with odd numbers and less equal skills. It is a good mix of exertion and sociability.

CANOEING

Canoeing is a good total body exercise if done with vigor in streams or white-water paddling (with possible hazards).

WATERSKIING

Waterskiing is good fun but noisy, and requires expensive equipment. It is not good for heart-diseased patients because of the anxiety and its largely isometic component.

HORSEBACK RIDING

Horseback riding is a fairly good exercise but is expensive and there is some chance of injury.

In all sports there is an ingredient of uncertainty. This ingredient is the way in which you engage in sports or exercise. You may play tennis but avoid running for balls or bowl by gently waving the ball toward the pins. On the other hand, if you go at it with vigor, using more calories, you will benefit much more.

Another important factor of any exercise program is time. If a person says, "I'm too busy, but when I find the time," he might as well forget it. A minimum of thirty minutes, four or five times a week is ideal—and not unreasonable. Sports require speed, skill, strength, and stamina. The young are more interested in the first. The last (stamina) adds to vigor, longevity, to the joy of living, to one's ability to do a day's work effectively, and to having enough pep left over to enjoy leisuretime.

STAYING IN SHAPE—MY OWN WAY

Fourteen years ago I decided that I must change my way of doing things. Busily engaged in taking care of sick people, my time was consumed by office work, hospital rounds, weekend calls, and so forth. My breathing was labored after walking up one flight of stairs and fatigue was my usual state. I had quit smoking four years earlier and weighed 175 pounds, 25 pounds more than my weight upon graduation from high school. I knew that I must change my ways.

I began a jogging program. Gradually I increased my mileage to three to four miles, three or four times weekly. It was not long before I weighed twenty pounds less, my breathing was much improved, and my energy was great.

I continued this program until last year. At that time I became interested in an experiment in physical conditioning conducted in Israel. It was found that brisk hiking was an effective way of getting into shape and staying that way. Furthermore, if a backpack was carried, with weights of 12-60 pounds, the conditioning process was greatly enhanced.

I believe the hiking program is as effective as the jogging. I now hike about forty minutes, three or four times each week, carrying a backpack weighing forty pounds. My weight remains normal. My eating habits include a considerable variety of fruits and vegetables with more fish and fowl than ever before and with rare use of red meat.

I made one other important change. Noting the tendency of chest, arm, and neck muscles to sag if unused, I started lifting weights. I found conventional weights to be unsatisfactory. They were bulky, hard to transport, and took up a lot of room. Knowing that lead was heavy, I bought a bag of lead shot used to reload shotgun shells. The bag was hard to handle without some alteration. I poured out the shot, had a canvas strap sewn onto the bag, and poured only twenty pounds back into the bag. This gave me a weight that I can carry on trips and one that will do the job if used frequently. I keep one in the office and one at home. My faithfulness in their use varies from once to three times daily for about ten minutes each time.

I am more careful to balance my life between work and play and make a special effort to stay strong physically, taking care to remember what Paul said to Timothy, "For bodily exercise profiteth little: but godliness is profitable unto all things, having promise of the life that now is, and of that which is to come" (1 Tim. 4:8).

MARATHON!

Living a Christian life is much like a marathon, maturity builds endurance but along the way pain, severe enough to threaten us, may make us want to quit.

In Hebrews 12, the writer exhorts us to make the commitment of a marathon runner—to finish the race and not quit: "Therefore, since we have so great a cloud of witnesses surrounding us, let us also lay aside every encumbrance, and the sin which so easily entangles us, and let us run with endurance the race that is set before us" (NASB).

At a certain point in marathon running, many runners come face to face with what has been called "The Wall." This seems to be a point where their energy resources are depleted and they can go no further. The best runners combat the wall by "staying loose" in their minds. They force their thoughts away from the problem onto other things like memories, or gaze into the distance searching for objects with which to identify. Other runners associatively monitor their body motions, watch their breathing, and ignore the wall.

Similarly, to concentrate on our difficulties is defeating; it might mean the loss of the race. Are you focusing on the pain, the problems in your personal life, or your relationships with others?

Or are you anticipating tomorrow's wall—future troubles? Jesus said in the Sermon on the Mount, "Do not be anxious for tomorrow; for tomorrow will care for itself. Each day has enough trouble of its own" (Matt. 6:34, NASB).

Rather, we are given the right focus in Hebrews 12 where we are told to fix our eyes on Jesus and run the race by faith. "Jesus, the author and perfector of faith, who for the joy set before Him endured the cross, despising the shame, and has sat down at the right hand of the throne of God" (v. 2, NASB), interceding for his followers. What a reassuring thought!

8
Eating to Live

Time and feeding had expanded that once romantic form; the black silk waistcoat had become more and more developed; inch by inch had the gold watch chain beneath it disappeared from the range of Tupman's vision, and gradually had the capacious chin encrouched upon the borders of the white cravat. —Dickens, (Pickwick Papers)

PERFECT EATING—AN ELUSIVE GOAL

We search, in part, for an understanding of how to eat through a look at our habits, and our cultural background. Some information, often misleading, is generated through television, newspapers, and magazines. Two facts, however, seem to be contradictory: (1) we live longer, in part, because of our varied, available, cleanly prepared foods; and (2) all this food is bad for us.

In a way, both of these statements are true. In our industrialized society we have the most varied, the cleanest and the most readily available food supply in the history of the world. But our affluence poses a problem in attitude and behavior regarding food. It is not a problem solved by genetic information passed from generation to generation. Our social development inadequately trains us to solve it. The problem is one of choice and the conviction that once we have made the choice of how to eat from such a range of food, we will stick with it. We are not born with the ability to choose wisely how we shall eat; it has to be learned. Even for those discriminating enough to seek answers about how to eat, the clamor of voices giving advice confuses the issue. Consequently, most people end up with a woefully inadequate list of information obtained from a friend, a fad diet, or a magazine article. Information about foods may be so confusing or unclear that we soon return to old practices and habits because it's easier. Consequently, the eating pattern is unchanged.

BREAKFAST—THE WAY TO START

It is a mystery why many people don't take time or make the effort to have an adequate breakfast. We are flooded with vitamin-fortified milk and cereals along with fruit of every variety in any season.

Surveys of work habits have shown the wisdom of eating breakfast. It pays off in alertness, efficiency, and reduced absentism because of illness. People who eat breakfast are shown to have increased longevity. Nutritionists have long advised starting the day with a balanced breakfast. With such advantages why do people skip breakfast?

When asked about breakfast, most patients who omit it will concentrate their answers in three areas: (1) they are too busy in the morning to eat; (2) they are not hungry; and (3) they are constipated in the morning.

Those with the first reason need to evaluate their time schedule and get up a bit earlier. There may be time to shop or watch the late show on TV but not enough time to revitalize the body for the day's problems.

A change in habits might help those with no appetite; change from heavy evening meals and evening snacks to light meals with no snacks. Starting with small portions at breakfast and gradually increasing them will ease the way to eating an adequate and balanced breakfast.

Constipation may result from poor bowel habits or disease of the intestinal tract. Many people will, however, benefit from breakfast cereals because of their high fiber content. This fiber assists in establishing a bowel movement reflex each morning.

Starting the day with a balanced breakfast gives a psychological boost as well as a physiological one. While we sleep, our bodies consume 500 to 600 calories for its internal work. During the period of fast, the energy stores have been emptied; our body needs refueling. If we do not replenish these energy stores, we may "drag along" feeling tired, headachy, or weak from low blood sugar.

NEW ENERGY EACH DAY

At night the body rests, but not entirely, for some work goes on day and night. Basic functions continue while we sleep: the heart beats, the blood flows through arteries and veins, and growth and repair of tissues goes on. We are kept alive and well through many vital "basal" functions which require "basal energy." The need of energy to fuel our basal requirments changes little throughout life.

Our basal state lasts about eight hours, and upon awakening, getting out of bed, washing, dressing, eating, talking, walking, and playing, we need additional energy. During the next sixteen hours or so, we may double our energy needs. These other activities may require as much or more energy than does our basal functions.

The wonderful scheme of nature is well shown when we analyze our energy needs and see how they are met. The sun serves as the basic source of energy but absorbing the sun's rays won't make you energetic. Our principal supply of energy comes from the foods we eat. These, in turn, have drawn their energy from the sun. The sun beams down on plants and this radiant energy is then changed to chemical energy by the process of photosynthesis. Fruits and vegetables absorb the sun's energy. Animals get energy through the hay and grain they eat. We get energy through eating fruits, vegetables, or meats.

We need different forms of energy but energy from food is chemical energy. It may be kept in this form for growth or changed to mechanical energy for muscle strength, to electrical energy for conduction of nerve impulses, and thermal energy to keep our bodies warm. Our bodies change one type of energy into another much like a power plant changes the water power in a river into electrical power. With these different forms of energy it is awkward to measure our energy needs in each form. A uniform measure is needed.

We have such a uniform measure in the calorie. This is a measure of energy as heat. In heating one kilogram of water (2.2 lbs.) from 15 to 16 degrees Celsius, one calorie is used up. But when we count calories in foods we are speaking of 1,000 of these small calories. So each food calorie is a K cal or 1,000 small calories. We are able then, by counting calories, to estimate the total potential energy in our foods.

We see then how we get energy and how we count energy but how is it released for use in the body? How does it make us strong enough to perform work or play ball when we need it?

The process is called metabolism. We eat food; it is absorbed throught the intestine and stomach wall in a chemical form and is then carried to our tissues where it is oxidized or burned. It is much like a furnace burning coal and releasing energy as heat. When we work or play, we become hot. Oxidation of food, combined with other chemical processes, is called metabolism. This is the process creating this heat.

It is possible to calculate the mechanical and electrical energy from calories. One pound of steak, for example, could run a one horse-power engine for two hours. A small radio could run for twenty-four hours on the energy in one slice of bread, but a two-inch slice of chocolate cake could run the same radio for one week. The calories in the same cake could generate heat equal to that in a stick of dynamite.

This emphasizes two important nutritional truths: (1) our foods contain an extraordinary amount of energy; and (2) calories do count.

If cake is equivalent to dynamite, why don't we explode when we eat cake? We know this doesn't happen and most of us have never considered it. Damage is prevented because we absorb and burn foods at a slow rate in many different parts of the body. Our built-in controls keep temperatures within a safe range. We need not worry about exploding.

If all foods are energy, why can't we just eat what strikes our fancy rather than selecting different kinds of food? The body's power is improved by selecting foods that provide an optimum plan of eating.

What does optimum nutrition mean? We must have the essential nutrients, which we get from a wide variety of foods, in a balanced combination. There must be enough variation of foodstuffs that our bodies have the energy and strength to resist life's daily stresses with a high degree of physical fitness and mental alertness. When we think of balance, we mean a plan that includes all the major food nutrients—proteins, carbohydrates, fats, vitamins, minerals, and fiber.

Balance also includes the amount of food you eat. If you work at a desk job and eat like a football player, you will become fat, storing the excess in your arms, legs, thighs, and so forth. On the other hand, the football player can't eat the amount a typist needs and expect to play well. He could draw some energy from stored fat or from body tissues, but this can't last very long. If the football player quits playing but eats as usual, he will gain weight. He is less active but eating too hearty.

Appetite is not well understood. We get hungry with an urge to eat but the signal to stop eating is not as clear—we may leave the table feeling stuffed. Thirst is a similar homeostatic mechanism and both of these work well when we are in nutritional balance. The signal to quit eating comes when we have a satisfied feeling of fullness. If our appetites rule our eating, we will get fat. It is vital that our wills control our appetites.

A diet is balanced, in amount, when we have enough food to guarantee the energy necessary to carry out our daily activities. We may need 1,200 calories for our basal requirements with another 1,200 calories for our work and play—2,400 calories will keep us in energy balance. Eating more will cause weight gain; eating less will cause a loss of weight.

The number of calories is not the only point to consider. If you need 2,400 calories every day, you could eat three six-ounce pieces of chocolate layer cake or 1½ pound steak and have your 2,000 calories. It would be ridiculous to eat like that. You need many types of foods to supply all the nutrients. The vitamins, minerals, and water in foods do not supply energy but are vital for good health. The best quality foods will not always mean the best tasting. It also means the wisest purchase of calories while maintaining a balanced diet. This brings better health and, surprisingly, often costs less.

METABOLISM

From the hour of birth to the time of death we have old cells which are dying or being repaired and new cells being formed.

All this takes raw materials and energy. Since we can't eat continuously, we must have a way to store energy in a form available as we need it.

Most of our immediate energy is supplied through carbohydrates, in the form of sugars. This energy may come from foods such as white or brown sugar or honey, either cooked into foods or in raw form. Energy from simple sugars is not as valuable as that from complex carbohydrates, such as potatoes, rice, or breads. Eating simple sugars shoots the blood sugar up too quickly with a swing downward that triggers appetites. We then look for something else to eat. On the other hand, complex carbohydrates are absorbed gradually with a gradual rise in the blood sugar. The blood sugar then falls gradually without the weak spells accompanying the eating of simple sugars.

We store energy in the form of fat. If we weigh too much and quit eating or "fast" in an effort to lose weight, our fat tissues are burned up to prevent the body's burning muscles and other tissues. The amount of energy, however, in fatty tissue is limited. If we continue to "fast," there will be some danger of injuring body tissues. Fasting as a form of dieting should be medically supervised.

Energy comes from proteins, carbohydrates, and fats but fats contain more than twice the energy of the other two:

>Proteins = 4 calories per gram or 120 calories per ounce.
>Carbohydrates = 4 calories per gram or 120 calories per ounce.
>Fats = 9 calories per gram or 270 calories per ounce.

Foods are usually a complex mixture of carbohydrates, fats and proteins, plus vitamins, minerals and water. The United States Department of Agriculture has provided a most useful book, *Composition of Foods,* which helps to accurately calculate the energy and nutrition in foods.

You simply cannot tell enough about foods by looking at the number of calories alone. For example, one tablespoon of sugar contains about fifty calories of energy in the form of sucrose, one-half boiled potato contains about fifty calories but also contains proteins, a trace of fat, complex carbohydrates, minerals, and vitamins. These two foods contain the same energy but differ in the amount of other nutrients.

Our bodies are built for action. Without action the muscles become flabby, blood flows sluggishly, the brain and other cells deteriorate. Each of our bodies' cells is an energy machine fighting for survival and trained with other cells fighting for the body's survival. To this end we eat.

In our energy conscious world, we hear of new forms of energy. Searchers for new energy have to bear in mind the first law of thermodynamics. We can neither create nor destroy energy. We only change it from one form to another. We have a constant amount of energy in several different forms. The total amount doesn't change, only the amount in one form over another.

Our bodies represent an energy system. We need to balance our output with out intake. If we're going to eat more, we must work harder to burn it or it piles up in the form of fat. The same law of thermodynamics applies; an unchanging law. The need of a proper balance of food cautions against "fad" diets and nutritional "trickery" but many stumble into this pitfall.

Many people treat the body as a yo-yo, dieting and stuffing, dieting and stuffing. This is tampering with nature and give us less than the best in energy and joy of life.

Our daily calorie needs do not have to be calculated to a precise caloric value. Each day is different and we are engaged in different activities. Tables showing average needs, calculated in calories, are useful if we allow an excess or reduction of about 10 percent to account for these individual and daily variations.

Table 1

Activity	Number of Hours	Man 154 lbs. Calories/Min	Total	Woman 128 lbs. Calories/Min	Total
Sleeping/resting	8	1.2	540	1	480
Very light work	12	1.8	1.300	1.2	900
Light work	3	3.3	600	2.5	450
Moderate work	1	5	300	4	240
	24		2,740		2,070

BODY SIZE ADJUSTMENTS

Bigger people require more food than smaller ones. Growing older usually brings decreased activity and the need to eat less. An adjustment must be made or we gain weight.

Most people, leading moderately active lives, will need about 15 calories per pound of weight per day. But this must be calculated from the weight they should have, not from their true weight, particularly if they are overweight. For example, if I weigh 165 pounds but should weigh 159—I need 159 x 15 = 2,310 calories each day.

This is a general calculation but will need to be altered depending on the amount of activity. If you usually work in an office, you will be able to use that guide but may need to eat more if you play tennis on a sunny afternoon. The heat and the increased activity require more energy.

ACTIVITY DOES COUNT

A piece of apple pie, too delicious to resist, will be burned up in twenty-three minutes of swimming but takes three hours of lying down resting or one and one-half hours of driving a car. A three-ounce steak will fuel one-half hour of swimming; one hour of fast walking; two hours of driving a car; three and one-half hours of rest or forty-seven minutes of tennis. The tennis player who trains and plays regularly will be able to play twice as long from the energy in that same steak. His muscles store and use energy more efficiently.

THE PRUDENT DIET

Several times every day each of us questions, what shall we eat? It is even a national question, discussed by the Select Nutrition Committee of the U. S. Senate. It is a question asked by food growers and food processors across the country. Our individual eating patterns are influenced by family backgrounds, traditions, impulsiveness, susceptibility to advertising, and our social contacts. The call for change in our eating patterns is clear. The route to take, the method to use, and the final goal are less clear. There are voices of agreement and disagreement to every suggestion.

The Senate Nutrition Subcommittee recommended these goals:

1. To avoid overweight, consume only as much energy (calories) as is expended; if overweight, decrease energy intake and increase energy expenditure.
2. Increase the eating of complex carbohydrates and "naturally occurring"

sugars from about 28 percent of energy intake to about 48 percent of energy intake.
3. Reduce the eating of refined and processed sugars by about 45 percent to account for about 10 percent of total energy intake.
4. Reduce overall fat consumption from approximately 40 percent to about 30 percent of energy intake.
5. Reduce saturated fat consumption to account for about 10 percent of total energy intake; and balance that with polyunsaturated and monounsaturated fats, which should account for about 10 percent of energy intake each.
6. Reduce cholesterol consumption to about 300 mg. a day.
7. Limit the intake of sodium by reducing the intake of salt to about 5 grams a day.

The goals suggest the following change in food selection and preparation:

1. Increase consumption of fruits and vegetables and whole grains.
2. Decrease consumption of refined and other processed sugars and foods high in such sugars.
3. Decrease consumption of foods high in total fat. Partially replace saturated fats, whether obtained from animal or vegetable sources, with polyunsaturated fats.
4. Decrease consumption of animal fat. Choose meats, poultry and fish which will reduce saturated fat intake.
5. Except for young children, substitute low-fat milk for whole milk, and low-fat dairy products for high-fat dairy products.
6. Decrease consumption of butterfat, eggs, and other high cholesterol sources. Allow premenopausal women, young children, and the elderly to have more cholesterol in order to obtain the nutritional benefits of eggs in the diet.
7. Decrease consumption of salt and foods with high salt content.

FATS

Such changes will spell the end to the high-fat American way of eating. Calorie, fat, and cholesterol consciousness has already convinced millions to switch to leaner cuts of meat and low-fat milk products and to replace lard, butter, and bacon fat with margarine and vegetable oils.

Many food producers now advertise their wares as "low cholesterol" or high in polyunsaturates. These claims need a careful look to prevent the unsuspecting consumer from being fooled by such labeling.

The advice we receive is not always sound. Consequently, many who think they are doing their hearts and arteries a favor by buying certain "vegetable" fats may be accomplishing little or nothing and may actually be hurting rather than helping. Some may avoid foods that could be safely eaten and enjoyed and others may substitute foods that are as bad or worse than the ones given up.

The decision to eat a lower fat diet, even relatively late in life, is supported by convincing evidence that it is helpful. Such a switch is more intelligently made if we know what kinds of fats are in the various foods we eat and the effect of these fats on the cholesterol that clogs our arteries.

The average American eats 42 percent of his food as fat, a figure much higher than primitive man (an estimated 10 percent). In the rush to reverse the risk of atherosclerosis and lower the fat in our diets, some have advocated "gimmick diets" that totally exclude or dangerously restrict all fats. Such advice runs counter to the opinions of many nutritionists and physicians that none of the essential nutrients in the diet should ever be totally excluded from the normal diet.

The word *fat* doesn't indicate one single substance that is either all good or all bad for us. Fats and fatty acids are complex foods that play a vital role in our survival and good health. When we eat fatty foods, we are consuming two basic types of fatty acids. Some fats become hard and congealed when cold, others are more fluid. The hard ones are saturated. The fluid types are composed, at least in part, of polyunsaturated fats, of which three are considered essential for good nutrition. These are called essential fatty acids. Though there are three of these, linoleic, linolenic, and arachidonic acids, linoleic is the most important one.

Fats play an important role in growth and reproduction. They also increase energy and are an important part of our skin barrier, protecting against water loss, and damage from radiation. We have no trouble in getting an adequate supply of linoleic acid from such foods as grain and seed oils, peanuts, poultry, and avocados. Some leafy green vegetables and legumes may contain up to 30 percent linoleic acid. Walnuts and safflower oil are very high with varying amounts in egg yolks, butter, corn oil, and animal tissues. Fish is strongly recommended as part of the diet because of the higher proportion of polyunsaturated acids than the amount contained in beef or chicken.

We know that fat is necessary for health but many studies have concluded that too much fat of the saturated type is harmful. The next important question is what kind and how much fat?

Table 2

Fat and Cholesterol Content of Foods

Food	Amount	Total Fat Percent	Saturated Fat Percent	Cholesterol Mg.
Meat Group				
Beef	3 oz.	25	12	80
Veal	3 oz.	12	6	80
Lamb	3 oz.	21	11	80
Pork, ham	3 oz.	26	10	80
Liver	3 oz.	5	1.3	225
Beef, dried	2 slices	6	3	18
Pork, sausage	2 links	44	16	45
Cold Cuts	1 slice	21	5	30
Frankfurters	1	35	18	30
Fowl	3 oz.	12	4	70
Eggs	1	12	4	253
Fish	3 oz.	9	1.5	75
Salmon & Tuna	¼ cup	17	5	—
Shellfish	3 oz.	6.5	2	135
Cheese	1 oz.	30	17	45
Cottage cheese	¼ cup	4	2	5
Peanut butter	2 T.	50	9	—
Peanuts	25	50	5	—
Fat Group				
Avocado	1/8	17	3	—
Bacon	2 strips	26	9	10
Butter	1 tsp.	80	46	12
Margarine	1 tsp.	80	22	—
Coconut oil	1 tsp.	100	88	—

Table 2 (continued)
Fat and Cholesterol Content of Foods

Food	Amount	Total Fat Percent	Saturated Fat Percent	Cholesterol Mg.
Corn oil	1 tsp.	100	10	—
Cottonseed oil	1 tsp.	100	26	—
Olive oil	1 tsp.	100	12	—
Peanut oil	1 tsp.	100	18	—
Safflower oil	1 tsp.	100	8	—
Sesame oil	1 tsp.	100	18	—
Soybean oil	1 tsp.	100	16	—
Vegetable fat	1 tsp.	100	20	—
Palm oil	1 tsp.	100	57	—
Sunflower oil	1 tsp.	100	11	—
Lard	1 tsp.	100	44	5
Half-andHalf	2 T.	12	6	12
Cream substitute dried	1 T.	25	15	—
Whipping cream	1 T.	36	21	18
Cream cheese	1 T.	25	20	18
Mayonnaise	1 tsp.	80	14	8
French dressing	1 T.	33	7	—
Nuts				
Almonds	5	58	5	—
Pecans	4	72	6	—
Walnuts	5	65	4	—
Olives	3	14	2	—
Milk Group				
Milk, whole	1 cup	4	2	27
2% milk	1 cup	2	1	15
Skim milk	1 cup			7
Cocoa (Skim)	1 cup	0.8	0.3	
Chocolate milk	1 cup	4	1	
Bread Group				
Bread	1 slice	3.2	1	
Biscuit	1	20	7	17
Muffin	1	10	2	16
Cornbread	1½" cube	13	4	16
Roll	1			

Table 2 (continued)
Fat and Cholesterol Content of Foods

Food	Amount	Total Fat Percent	Saturated Fat Percent	Cholesterol Mg.
Pancake	1-4" diam.	7	2	38
Waffle	1	10	3	28
Sweet roll	1	23	7	25
French toast	1 slice	12	6	130
Doughnut	1	20	4	27
Cereal, cooked	2/3 cup	1		
Crackers, salted	6	10	3	
Popcorn, unbuttered	1 cup	5	0.7	
Potatoes				
potato chips	1 oz. bag	40	10	
French fried in corn oil	10	12	0.8	
in hydrogenated fat	10	12	3.2	
Mashed	½ cup	4	1	
Soup, cream	½ cup	4	1	
Dessert				
Ice milk	½ cup	3	2	5
Ice cream	½ cup	12	7	.43
Sherbet	⅓ cup	1	0.8	
Low-fat cookies	5	10	2	
Cake	1 piece	30	4	40
Fruit pie	1/6 pie (9")	9	3	11
Miscellaneous				
Gravy	¼ cup	23	18	18
White sauce	¼ cup	14	6	29
Coconut	1 oz.	36	31	
Chocolate sauce	1 oz	13	7	

Even before the recommendations of the Senate Committee on Nutrition, the American Heart Association and other health organizations recommended no more than 30-35 percent of calories as fat compared to the 40-45 percent currently consumed by the average American. Polyunsaturated fats should be in a ratio of 2 to 1 over saturated fats. In addition, they recommended a cholesterol intake of less than 300 mg. per day for prudent eating.

SOURCES OF FAT IN THE AMERICAN DIET

Fat comes from these groups of foods:
1. milk and milk products
2. meat, fish, and poultry
3. eggs
4. grain products
5. fats and oils

The lists in table four give detailed information about the fat contained in many commonly used foods.

CARBOHYDRATES

The carbohydrates are the most fundamental of all foodstuffs. The energy we use to move, to perform work, and to live is mostly supplied from carbohydrates. Since the dawn of history they have provided the most abundant and the least expensive sources of food energy in man's diet. For this reason alone, they naturally form the largest part of the diet of most people, varying from 45 percent to 70 percent in different parts of the world. For us the most important carbohydrates are starch, sugar, and fiber. We have gradually decreased fiber and starch in favor of sugar. A hundred years ago, Europeans ate about 4¼ pounds of sugar per person each year. By comparison, we Americans now eat an average of 128 pounds of sugar per person each year.

Sugar, such as we find in the sugar bowl, comes primarily from sugar cane and sugar beets. Sugar in soft drinks comes primarily from corn. All carbohydrates are made from combinations of the basic sugars, glucose, and fructose. These two sugars, called monosaccharides are used to build other more complex carbohydrates such as disaccharides, of which sucrose (ordinary granular sugar) is one and polysaccharide, complex chains of which fiber and starch are the best known.

Our tastes for sweets causes us to eat more simple sugars but fewer complex carbohydrates. At the turn of the century, we were eating 70 percent of our carbohydrates as starches but this is now only 47 percent. Starches are of importance nutritionally, due to their characteristics. Potatoes, for example, are composed of glucose and fructose but they do not taste sweet; they hide the sweet taste of the sugar molecule of which they are made.

Eating refined sugars causes a yo-yo like effect on our production of insulin. Simple sugars, absorbed quickly, cause the blood sugar to increase rapidly, insulin is secreted by the pancreas; the blood sugar falls and we experience a weak feeling which we may combat by eating "something sweet," and the cycle starts all over again. This is one way excessive weight is gained. On the other hand, absorption of sugars from starches and complex carbohydrates is smooth and even, without the roller-coaster effect on insulin and blood sugar.

Only a few foods of animal origin contain carbohydrates. Eggs and shellfish have small amounts. Milk is exceptional in that over one third of the solid milk is lactose, a disaccharide commonly called milk sugar.

CARBOHYDRATES AND DISEASE

The relationship between carbohydrates and disease is just now being appreciated. This relationship or link is inextricably bound to the change in our eating habits from a high-fiber to a low-fiber diet. The process of refining grain foods and sugars is part of the pattern, as well as the drop in consumption of potatoes and whole grains. The evidence that there is a link is not conclusive but highly suggestive.

Epidemiological studies of the distribution of a certain disease in a particular geographical location may lead to an understanding of the cause. For example, in 1854 London was struck by an outbreak of cholera, and hundreds of townspeople died while city authorities searched for the cause of the epidemic. Finally, Dr. John Snow noticed that people who had come down with cholera shared one characteristic: they all drew their drinking water from the same public water pump. Dr. Snow traced the water to its source and found that it was drawn from the River Thames just below the spot where the raw sewage flowed into the stream. This was a classic epidemiological study. He used the geographical distribution of a disease to help him identify its cause and apply preventive measures.

has been misunderstood and largely neglected. Fiber's importance and definition in health is now being sought, as well as the influence of processing.

CHARACTERISTICS OF FIBER

The most important characteristic of fiber is its ability to decrease the amount of water, cholesterol, and bile salts that is absorbed from the intestine. Bile salts, produced in the liver, are of importance because of their role in carrying fat from the intestine into the bloodstream. Fiber affects the absorption of these substances in two ways. First, it passes through the bowel like a sponge, absorbing the bile salts and cholesterol along with the water. Second, it hastens the passage of digested food material out of the bowel, reducing the time of absorption through the intestinal wall.

Fiber, through its effect on intestinal bacteria, reduces the amount of toxic material that comes in contact with the bowel wall. Finally, fiber, through its capacity to supply bulk, makes a person feel satisfied more quickly than low-fiber food with the same calorie value. Fibrous foods take longer to chew, forcing slower eating, which tends to lower food intake.

FIBER AND DIVERTICULOSIS

New ideas about fiber have already resulted in a change in the method of treating diverticulosis. Dr. Burkitt feels that this common disease of the large intestine, in which small pockets develop on the bowel wall, is caused by increased straining from constipation. The basic problem, low fiber in the diet, causes reduction of bulk because of less water in the bowel. Doctors, in treating diverticulosis, have changed from low-fiber diets to high-fiber diets with reduced abdominal pain and distention.

FIBER AND CANCER OF THE BOWEL

Cancer of the bowel occurs four times as often in Denmark as in Finland. High fat diets are suspected to cause cancer because of the production of toxic materials as the fat is digested. The people in Denmark and Finland, however, eat about the same amount of fat. Dr. R. MacLeuman, of the International Agency for Research on

Cancer in Lyon, France, reports that Finns eat 80 percent more fiber than Danes do, mostly in the form of rye foods. Other studies support the finding of increased cancer of the colon in people who eat low-fiber diets.

Certain intestinal bacteria, during the process of digestion, produce chemicals, known as carcinogens, which irritate the intestinal wall. Frequent, repeated irritations over many years is though to be necessary to produce cancer in the intestinal wall. Fibrous foods are thought to prevent this is three ways; increased water, diluting the carcinogens; decreased contact of these carcinogens with the intestinal wall through increased speed of elimination of food material through the intestinal tract; and production of increased acid, diminishing the action of the intestinal bacteria.

FIBER AND HEART DISEASE

A similar mix of factors is probably at work in the association of low-fiber diets with coronary heart disease. Dr. J. N. Morris of the London School of Hygiene and Tropical Medicine studied diet habits and coronary heart disease in a group of 337 middle-aged men. Those men eating a high-fiber diet were less prone to develop heart disease. The fiber from cereals, not fruits, vegetables or nuts, seemed to be more protective.

One possible explanation for Dr. Morris's observation is that fiber, by building cholesterol and bile salts in the intestine, helps to reduce the level of fats in the blood. Investigators at the U. S. Department of Agriculture's Human Nutrition Laboratory in Grand Forks, North Dakota, recently substantiated this explanation by reporting that cereal fiber reduced the levels of cholesterol and low-density lipoprotein (the harmful portion of cholesterol) in the blood of fifteen healthy men. These researchers, like the British investigators, found that not all sources of dietary fiber were equally effective in reducing blood-fat levels; cereal fiber was better than that of fruits or vegetables.

The research at Grand Forks also found that when the fat levels of these volunteers dropped, their blood sugar curves improved. This suggests that high-fiber diets are important in yet another of the chronic degenerative diseases—diabetes. It is believed, as mentioned previously, that starches low in fiber and simple sugars are more rapidly absorbed and converted to glucose than high-fiber complex carbohydrates. The glucose enters the bloodstream quickly, increasing demands on the pancreas to produce insulin, a situation that may predispose a person to developing diabetes.

Slowing absorption of glucose from the intestine may explain the improved glucose levels in the blood and also suggests that fiber may be used to treat diabetes as well as to prevent it. Drs. Miranda and Horowitz at the University of Chicago found that the blood-sugar levels of seven diabetes dropped from 13 to 57 percent when they switched from eating a low-fiber diet to one with a high-fiber content. Two of these patients had dramatic falls in their blood sugar levels requiring a decrease in their daily insulin dose in order to avoid insulin shock.

FIBER—HOW MUCH; WHICH FOODS?

According to Dr. Peter Van Soest of Cornell University, whose pioneering work in fiber has led to its redefinition, the essential components of fiber are cellulose, which gives fiber its threadlike quality; hemicellulose, which imparts toughness to cell walls; lignin which provides the fragility, and stiffness that make plants woody and pectin, found especially in apples and oranges.

Dr. Denis Burkitt recommends eating 22 grams (about 3/4 oz.) of dietary fiber as a daily supplement. This amount of fiber is to be eaten in addition to the usual variety of vegetables, fruits, and nuts in a balanced diet. It is most easily obtained from bran cereals. The fiber in bran is only one third digested in fifteen hours; vegetable fiber is almost completely digested in this time. The pectin in apples and oranges coats the lining of the intestine, assisting the fiber in binding chemicals, increasing rapid movement of intestinal contents, and possibly lowering cholesterol levels in the blood.

Knowledge of the role of fiber in the prevention or treatment of a particular disease will require further investigation in future years. It seems prudent, for the present, to concentrate on the water-binding capacity fiber. Fruits and vegetables already contain high water content, consequently large amounts of these foods are required to provide the amount of fiber available in cereals. Useful steps to improve bowel function would involve a change from white bread to bread made entirely with whole wheat flour, the daily addition of one to two heaping tablespoonsful of Miller's bran or all bran in soup or cereal, a choice of fiber-rich breakfast cereals, increased consumption of potatoes, and a general reduction of foods containing sugar and white flour.

Dr. Burkitt feels that many of the degenerative diseases that show up in adult life often start in childhood and the effects of a low-fiber diet are not limited to the later years. Degenerative diseases are likely to have multiple causes but if we determine the minimum dietary changes necessary to shift our children to a safer pattern, we will have taken a major step in preventive medicine. Lack of fiber in the diet appears to be one of the important causes of degenerative diseases that is easily corrected.

PROTEINS

In spite of misconceptions about proteins, we don't have to worry about getting enough. They come to us from any living thing we eat—from plants, which make their protein from the soil and from animals which make their protein from eating plants. In any reasonable diet we get enough and in many cases eat twice as much as we need.

Although all living matter contains proteins, some foods contain more than others. Cabbage and lettuce are only 1 or 2 percent protein but peas and beans contain as much as 25 percent. Meat, eggs, fish, and cheese are very rich in protein—20 to 30 percent. Cereals like wheat, corn, and rice contain less but are good sources. Potatoes, carrots, and beets contain only about 5 percent. Carrots, cereal, steak, and liver represent a wide variety of foods but they all contain protein. Proteins are formed from twenty basic units—the amino acids—in varying proportions. These twenty units, arranged in different sequences, account for several thousand different kinds of proteins in foods.

Our bodies lose and therefore need to replace about 40 grams (1½ ounces) of protein a day. Since we eat more protein than we need, our caloric intake from protein will be about 12 percent rather than 5 percent. Children use this to build new flesh, blood, and tis-

EATING TO LIVE

sues. Adults use it for replacement and repair of broken down tissues of the body.

Milk and eggs have the highest "biological value" as protein, but if we eat a varied diet we will get enough, even if the value is lower. We may eat foods containing proteins with an average biological value of 75 percent, as compared to the white of an egg, which is 100 percent. Since we eat more than we need, 75 percent is more than sufficient.

CHEAPEST WAYS TO GET PROTEIN

The Agriculture Department has some help for people who want to cut food costs without sacrificing nutrition.

Using Bureau of Labor Statistics figures collected in September 1978, the USDA has calculated the cost of 40 grams of protein from different sources. Dry beans were the least expensive protein source at 41 cents a pound. It takes a little less than one-half pound to obtain 40 grams of protein, leading to a protein cost of 20 cents.

At the other end of the scale were lamb chops at $3.09 per pound. It takes a little less than two thirds of a pound to get 40 grams of protein, so that would cost $1.90.

Other sources of protein and the cost to obtain 40 grams included:

Peanut butter	$.36
Beef liver or enriched white bread	.36
Hamburger	.40
Eggs	.42
Chicken	.46
Milk	.50
Turkey	.52
Pork	.56
Beef chuck roast	.62
American processed cheese or tuna fish	.66
Ham	.74
Frankfurters	.84
Liverwurst	.94
Salami	.98
Sardines	1.08
Sirloin steak	1.14
Bologna	1.20
Pork chops	1.30

Haddock 1.34
Veal cutlets 1.36
Pork sausage 1.52
Porterhouse steak 1.70
Bacon 1.78

EATING — A SOCIAL DILEMMA: PLEASURE AND STRUGGLE

Eating and drinking are paradoxically and, to some degree, diabolically pleasant. The pleasure is greater when food and drink are taken with friends and family. This results in normal people with normal appetites becoming pudgy because of their stopping off for the odd drink with a friend, finishing off a meal in a restaurant with dessert they really didn't want, eating at reunions and parties just for the fun of it, and adopting a "vending machine mentality" twice daily at coffee-break time.

This adds the subtle pressures of social demands and inner psychological demand to appetite and habit in the struggle to keep our eating within reason.

It is hard to decline an offer of coffee and cake or cookies from a neighbor, son, daughter-in-law, or grandparents. In our society this unites our feelings of friendship and kinship. But, in other societies—Africa and the Middle East, the customs of eating greatly influence conduct among friends.

We may conform to other societal standards which involve eating and drinking, attending office parties, even eating three meals a day at a set time. The congenial atmosphere and the desire to behave tactfully and not offend the host leads to overeating when we go back for second or third helpings.

In bygone days when food was scarce and valuable, it represented a true sign of friendship, but our customs have not kept pace with our oversupply of food. We continue to press food on each other in social gatherings. This process requires a thoughtful alertness to what we serve as well as what and how much we accept when attending social gatherings.

Advertising, a newer social pressure, is used to stimulate our basic urges for happiness by relating them to food and, at the same time, to play on our unhealthy attitudes to food that may have been acquired in childhood. We console a child with food after a fall or while fretting or as an inducement to do a chore. Later, this may act as a conditioned reflex, so that we eat when frustrated or depressed. Food then becomes a subconscious attempt to recreate a sense of security. It fails, but the food makes fatness, fatness makes discontent, discontent makes depression, depression causes eating—a vicious cycle is established.

There are two ways of negating some of the stimuli which lead to overeating: (1) keep a strict diary of what you eat, when, and where; and (2) avoid automatic eating. The first of these will give a clearer picture of the internal and external motives for eating. Anger, frustration, recurring situations can be recognized and avoided or confronted and resolved. Eating automatically leads many people to an overweight state. They do not necessarily enjoy their food. They eat familiar foods and those that are easiest to prepare—which are, all too often, the foods which cause gain of weight. Bread, bought cookies, and cakes need no preparation; frying foods is less difficult but gives more calories. It is far better to take more interest in cooking, creating more difficult but healthier dishes—changing to an attitude of critical and alert eating. If you're going to gain weight, make sure it's from something so delicious that you just can't resist—not on junk.

FOOD FADS AND DIETARY FOOLISHNESS

An endless succession of dietary regimes appears in the media, each purporting to be the ultimate solution. These permutations of fuel mixtures range from the impossible to the ridiculous. If they have any common features, it is that they make elaborate promises of success, they understate the rigors of adherence, and they try to place the decision for dietary restriction in the hands of the dieter. . . . The other common feature of reducing regimes is their commercialism—someone stands to make money from their promotion (George V. Mann, Sc.D., M.D., Associate Professor of Medicine and Biochemistry at Vanderbilt University, in *The New England Journal of Medicine*).

Dr. Mann's statement doesn't include the most impelling reason to steer clear of unsound diets—they could kill you! It is probable that more people try fad diets than sound ones; a testimony to the intractable nature of the overweight problem and to the unwillingness of the more than 60 million Americans afflicted with this problem to recognize that no shortcut will get the job done.

Weight loss schemes abound. They are traded, bought, discussed, and given away in an endless manner. But they are not analyzed carefully and reaching to "shed those ugly pounds of fat forever" becomes the stimulus to be off on yet another search for the real slim you that is enclosed within that fat.

But there are hazards to this careless approach. Some of the more popular diets and their hazards follow:

LIQUID PROTEIN DIETS

Dr. Robert Linn's book, *The Last Chance Diet*, popularized the concept of the modified fast, a diet not intended for general public use, but to be used only under strict medical supervision. This was aligned with the birth of a new elixir, Prolinn.

Prolinn was initially made from the hides, tendons, and bones of cattle, laced with trytophan, an essential amino acid, flavored to hide the abominable taste, and promoted at considerable cost.

But that's not the worst part. We awakened to the fact that not only was there danger in the uncontrolled use of this concept, but that an estimated 3 million people had tried the diet.

Some overdid it and died. Many people suffered with tragic effects. Others became ill of heart irregularities, potassium imbalance, skin changes, and hair loss. Even with these serious consequences, the concept is still being promoted, oftentimes with slight modifications, and there are still susceptible, searching people buying and trying this approach to weight loss.

LOW CARBOHYDRATE DIETS

These come in many guises—the Stillman Diet, Calories Don't Count Diet, Drinking Man's Diet, Air Force Diet, and others. In all of these, the idea is to eat few or no carbohydrates—sugars and starches—which means no grains or fruits and few vegetables, as well as no candy, cake, bread, and the like.

This leaves fat and protein to supply the body's needs. While the Stillman Diet cautions against high-fat foods, the others say you can eat all the fat you want. Many sources of protein—meat and dairy products—are also high in saturated fats and cholesterol. Thus, these diets add the problems of promoting clogging of the arteries and heart disease.

The loss of appetite accompanying the use of these diets comes from a sharp rise in compounds called ketones in the blood. These result from the body's inability to completely burn the excessive fat and protein. The resulting ketosis causes nausea, vomiting, weakness, dizziness, lowered blood pressure, and the danger of kidney failure if there is any kidney damage.

Other hazards of these diets include disturbances in heart rhythm, excess uric acid in the blood, and, in pregnant women, impairment of brain development in the unborn child.

The high protein creates an additional hazard as the waste products are eliminated by the kidney. Unknown, mild kidney disease is catapulted into uremic poisoning by the added load of nitrogenous wastes.

Calcium depletion and softness of the bones may occur along with symptoms resembling scurvy—from Vitamin C deficiency—when a high protein diet omits fruits and vegetables.

MACROBIOTIC AND OTHER DIETS

Although the basic macrobiotic diet is reasonably well balanced, those who progress to the so-called high levels risk severe malnutrition. Subsisting solely on rice, the dieter may feel full but is actually starved, suffering from protein, vitamin, and mineral deficiencies that can cause serious illness and death.

Total fasting, modified fasting, and alternate day fast should be medically supervised to prevent those complications known to occasionally occur—heart failure, small intestinal obstruction, kidney failure, diabetic acidosis, and nutritional deficiencies of Vitamin C and certain amino acids.

REDUCING DRUGS

The dangers of using reducing drugs are real. The evidence that they are effective is lacking. Tolerance to a given dose quickly develops and an increased dose or continued dose can cause psychological addiction, impaired judgment, and paranoid behavior.

Thyroid hormones increase the body's metabolic rate but are dangerous, especially if heart disease is present. They are unproven in producing a permanent weight loss.

Diuretics rid your body of water, not fat. The water is replaced and the weight is regained. Careless use of diuretics can cause weakness, dizziness, and imbalance of the body's internal minerals, sodium and potassium.

Human chorionic gonadotrophic (HCG) is promoted in weight reduction clinics as an injection to rid the body of fat. Its safety has not been established but it has been shown to be useless in weight control.

In summary, diet-aid gimmicks—liquids, powders, pills, or others—are generally of no real value for successful, long-term weight control. For the severely obese person, with health impaired as a result of the obesity, a modified fast, under proper medical supervision, may be worth considering.

For most overweight people, however, a nutritionally balanced diet that allows a gradual weight loss and emphasizes long-term modification of eating patterns is the safest approach. Self-help groups, such as TOPS (Take Off Pounds Sensibly) and Weight Watchers often achieve results that match any available medical treatment for obesity.

9
God's Nature—Healing

And he cried to the Lord; and the Lord showed him a tree, and he threw it into the water, and the water became sweet. There the Lord made for them a statute and an ordinance and there he proved them, saying, "If you will diligently hearken to the voice of the Lord your God, and do that which is right in his eyes, and give heed to his commandments and keep all his statutes, I will put none of the diseases upon you which I put upon the Egyptians; for I am the Lord, your healer" (Ex. 15:25,26 RSV).

Joe Thompkins, our patient who died from a diseased heart, sought healing, only to have it escape him. His chest pains indicated advanced disease. His disease, however, having started in childhood, was far advanced when he became sick. There was no chance of cure of his coronary vascular disease at that point but there was a chance of improvement if he had followed instructions. He was advised to quit smoking, lose weight, and begin an exercise program. He found these changes in life-style too drastic.

LIVING YET DEAD

Joe was in some ways, an example of two significant circumstances which bring disappointment and discouragement to a doctor's work: (1) the patient who has relief of the physical aspects of his problems but continues to show the same mental attitude of the sickness. There is no enthusiasm for life. Everything is defeating. Life is a drag; and (2) the patient who has a problem which can be overcome largely through his own effort but who fails to mount that effort, expressing instead the same feelings of defeat and despair. It is as though there is nothing to live for. Those things which are usually important, such as family, happiness and wealth, have become unattractive. In many ways this is the same as death: his need—a spiritual recognition of the role of the soul and spirit in controlling his life.

Understanding, reacting, responding, knowing, and loving are capacities of the soul. The soul enables a deeper relationship than the physical one. If that relationship blossoms into a deep and lasting affection and commitment, we have topped the capacity of the soul for love.

The spirit of man is unmistakably unique. Without it we would have no capacity to know and enjoy God. It is this capacity which marks the lowest man, elevating him above the highest animal. For, even in this day of disbelief, skepticism, agnosticism, and atheism every person has an inherent sense of the reality of God. This longing for God is found in the most primitive tribes in the form of objects of worship. More sophisticated societies may substitute money, ambition, hobbies, or a person as an object of worship.

We see then that people operate on three planes: physically with the body, socially with the soul, and spiritually with the spirit. Just as we have the capacity to operate on all three planes simultaneously, we also have the capacity to function on just two planes. If the body functions normally, this doesn't mean that the spirit is functioning perfectly. Thus, a person may be evidently physically alive and spiritually dead at the same moment. Paul stated it well, "She that liveth in pleasure is dead while she liveth" (1 Tim. 5:6). Jesus startled his disciples by saying "I am come that they might have life" (John 10:10), but he was talking of living persons. How could he give persons who were physically alive more physical life than they already had? Jesus was emphasizing the need for spiritual life. How did he make the diagnosis? Just as a physician diagnoses a condition by observation, Jesus observed the actions, listened to the talk, learned of the objects of their affection, and watched their appetites. He then diagnosed the soul and heart of man: "Your souls aren't harmed by what you eat, but by what you think and say!" (Mark 7:15-16, TLB). "And then he added, 'It is the thought-life that pollutes. For from within, out of men's hearts, come evil thoughts of lust, theft, murder, adultery, wanting what belongs to others, wickedness, deceit, lewdness, envy, slander, pride, and all other folly. All these vile things come from within; they are what pollute you and make you unfit for God' " (vv. 20-22, TLB).

But the lack of appetite for God is a major symptom of spiritual deadness. Other parts of the syndrome of spiritual death are: (1) no hunger for the Bible; (2) complete absence of spiritual activity, and (3) inability to measure and evaluate life on a spiritual basis. If our muscles are not used, they atrophy and we become weak. If our souls are not used, we withdraw and become a recluse or are antisocial. If we have spiritual death, we may feel a void or be conscious that our lives are not full since we are made to enjoy communion with God but may suffer from inactivity in our spiritual life. It is not surprising that we may say, "Something is missing from life."

Recently I had a young man tell me that he thought he had "rabies." He was nauseated, couldn't eat, couldn't sleep, had difficulty swallowing, and had a feeling of numbness in his arms. He had been bitten by a wild raccoon three months before. The raccoon was lying in the road and appeared dead. He picked it up and the warmth of his car revived it. It climbed under his dash and as he reached for it, he was bitten. He threw the raccoon out of his car in his anger over the bite. The wound was slow to heal and, as he showed me, left an ugly scar. He didn't bother to see a doctor until three months after the bite.

This was a tough dilemma. There was no way of telling if he had rabies, except to biopsy his brain or to await the inevitable progression of the disease if he had it. Since rabies has an incubation period of one year, I recommended rabies vaccine. He declined it. On the second visit, his mother came. She told of earlier years, his involvement with drugs, his divorce from his first wife at age twenty-one, and his poor employment record. His father lived apart from them but several weeks earlier he had read to the son the symptoms of rabies from a medical book.

The picture became clearer. I felt that the young man had "pseudorabies" (false rabies). I suggested to him that since rabies was usually fatal, with only one or two cases having survived it, that his greatest need was a spiritual need. He was somewhat receptive and promised to consider it. He returned in ten days with the same symptoms but no fever, chills, or other new symptoms. He had begun reading the Bible and praying; his sleep was improved. He has not returned since that visit, but there is no record of death from rabies in either of the local hospitals.

Cases such as this illustrate the immense control of the emotions, generated through the mind, in producing symptoms in the body. On the second visit, this patient has a rash which I thought was due to his worrying mind. It was on the same visit that he showed his anger as he said, "Man, here I am dying of rabies and you're not doing a thing." His chronic brooding led to a faulty attitude. The next step was a faulty reaction: self-pity.

This young man was a victim of a poorly developed personality. He had worked a little, divorced early, used drugs, and now suffered from a psychosomatic illness triggered by the raccoon bite. His need was a spiritual healing. His illness, begun in childhood, would have been far more successfully prevented than treated.

Patients with fears, worries, and feelings of being unable to cope with the stresses of life, visit doctors daily. Some acknowledge the shallowness of their spiritual lives. Others do not agree that their problem is a spiritual void. Many lives have a deadness at the center but there is not agreement on its cause or its cures. Counselors recommend life patterned after a good example; others emphasize encouragement. Yet others will suggest a change of environment or an educational pursuit as the solution.

All of these may help in certain circumstances but spiritual death is countered only by spiritual life. Our personalities develop as we experience life and our consciousness builds one experience upon another. We can train our consciousness to further our spiritual development by using our minds to think of the basic principle of the Christian life.

THIRSTY CHRISTIANS

God expects us to behave rationally. He created us and our rationality as part of his divine image. To deny our rationality is to deny our humanity, to become less than human beings. Scripture forbids us to behave like horses or mules which are "without understanding" (Ps. 32:9, RSV). We are commanded instead to be "mature" in our understanding (1 Cor. 14:20). The Bible constantly tells us that Christian life and Christian thinking are impossible without the Christian use of our minds.

When Jesus said, "I have finished the work which thou gavest me to do," he signified a basic fact of Christianity as well as the basis of Christian thinking. The work of which he spoke was the redemption of the human race, making it possible for every person to establish communion with God, all ordered by Jesus' death on the cross.

SUFFERING

Anyone who attempts to deal with the problems of suffering in a brief writing lays himself open to the charge of rashness, if not of sheer folly. On the other hand, those who, down through the years, have written, lectured, or spoken on suffering, are aware of the great response of those addressed. Many raise questions which refuse to be silenced and often they are questions which are a barrier to faith. If Jesus, as he was suspended on the cross, sent heavenward the anguished cry, "My God, my God, why . . . ?" it is hardly a surprise that a similar cry is wrung from those like ourselves from time to time, some more often than others.

I once cared for a young man in his early twenties. He had noted the growth of a lymph node in his neck for two months. This was biopsied a few days after he came to the office, and the pathologists report confirmed my suspicion that this was a malignant lymphoma. He was referred to a medical center for removal of his spleen. During the operation, a search was made for other enlarged lymph nodes and none were found. He recovered from his surgery and the cancer chemotherapy teams recommended that he be given treatments with four different drugs. These were started but were not continued as strictly as recommended because of the young man's depression and hopeless attitude. His spirits brightened somewhat when improvement was noted in the size of the lymph nodes. His attitude eventually completely changed.

We continued treatment over the next two years, during which period he felt well enough to work and enjoy a fairly normal life. His parents did not do as well as he. The father failed to acknowledge the seriousness of the problem, preferring to deny that his son had a potentially fatal disease. The mother was a nurse and her training gave her insight into the problem. During the course of his illness, she sought to renew her relationship with God, seeking his comfort and love.

I was aware of the fact that my young friend's lymph nodes had never become normal size, in spite of the chemotherapy. This was an ominous sign, which signaled that the disease, though quiet during those two years, was bound to rear its ugly head at some future date.

It began with fever, chills, cough, and headaches. An X-ray showed patchy pneumonia. He was hospitalized for treatment with intravenous antibiotics. The infection quickly spread from his lungs to the bloodstream, causing a fall in blood pressure and other symptoms of infectious shock. Our attempts at treatment were met with one complication after another. Death was not long in coming.

His mother was anguished but in her recently renewed faith, said, "I must accept it. It is the will of God."

SUFFERING AS THE WILL OF GOD

The mother called her son's death "the will of God" though I had been using every medical means I knew to save his life. If I had been successful, we would have thanked God with deep feeling that in the recovery of that son, his will had been done. When sadness, disease, calamity, or suffering of any kind overtakes people, they sometimes say with resignation, "God's will be done," when, as a matter of fact, just the opposite of his will has been done. When Jesus walked the hills of Palestine healing men's bodies and gladdening hearts, he was doing God's will, not undoing or defeating it.

The cross offers us a supreme illustration of God's will.

1. It was not the intentional will of God, surely, that Jesus should be crucified, but that he should be followed. If Israel had understood and received his message, repented of its sins, and recognized his kingdom, the world's history would have been different. Rather than say the crucifixion was the will of God, we should remember that it was the will of evil men.

2. But Jesus was faced with circumstances brought about by evil and was thrust into the dilemma of running away or of being crucified. Then, in those circumstances, the cross was his Father's will. It

was in this sense that Jesus said, "Not what I will, but what thou wilt."

3. We must look beyond circumstances to discover God's ultimate will. This means that the high goal of man's recovery to a unity with God, a goal which would have been reached by God's intentional plan had it not been frustrated, will still be reached through his circumstantial will. Circumstantial evil is not able to defeat God or prevent his ultimate goal.

God has an intentional purpose for the life of my young patient but the disease afflicting his body cut across God's plan. In this case, death was caused by infectious germs. I suppose God is responsible for the creation of germs, even the germs of disease. Why they are created I don't know. I think we could do without them but they may serve a useful purpose about which we know nothing. These germs invaded a body, the resistance of which the evil of cancer had lowered, and the result was a fatal disease. That disease you can call, if you like, the circumstantial will of God. But it is the will of God only within the circumstances created by evil.

We can identify two parts to the circumstantial will of God—one in the natural realm and the other in the spiritual. The cross of Christ again vividly portrays these two expressions:

1. Given the circumstances placed on Jesus by evil men, it was God's will that Jesus should be betrayed, taken, crowned with thorns, crucified, and left in the sun to die. The laws of the universe, which are themselves an expression of God's will, were not set aside for Jesus, the beloved Son. The laws which govern the hammering in of nails held on the day of crucifixion in just the same way they do now when we nail boards to make a house. If a typhoon sweeps across a tropical island inhabited by Christians and non-Christians, the homes and lives of both are swept away by the force. If a strong arm wields a hammer against the head of a nail, that nail can pierce the flesh of the hand of even the Son of God. The laws of the universe are operating, and because those laws are an expression of God's will, you may, if you like, call these things the will of God, but only in a limited sense. The forces of nature carry out their functions and are not changed or deflected when they are used by the forces of evil.

When Christ's flesh was torn on the cross, the laws of God, in regard to pain, operated just as they do when a hand is cut with a knife today. Christ accepted that as part of the ordering of the universe which was the will of a wise, holy, and loving God. He did not fling it back at God that it was unfair that the laws should operate in his case because he was God's Son.

2. But the circumstantial will of God contains a second element. The first we may call natural and the second spiritual. Christ could have submitted to the dreadfulness of the crucifixion with resignation, but he did not. He took hold of the situation. Given those circumstances which evil had produced, it was also God's will that Jesus could not just die like a trapped animal, but that he would so react to evil, positively and creatively, as to wrest good out of evil circumstances. The cross then becomes not just a symbol of capital punishment similar to the hangman's noose, but a symbol of the triumphant use of evil in the cause of the holy purposes of God. In other words, by doing the circumstantial will of God, we open up the way to God's ultimate triumph with no loss of anything of value to ourselves.

Let us turn to the question of sickness in the light of the preceding comments. The Christian minister is confronted as he does his hospital visiting, by the question as to whether the onset of disease is the will of God. The answer is undoubtedly no. The will of God for man is perfect health. Other things being equal, God can use a body free from disease more effectively than a diseased body. If Jesus had been lame or diabetic or sufferd from tuberculosis, he would not have been a greater spiritual asset in his ministry. But there is a will of God within the evil circumstances of disease and sickness. Everyone who suffers has the chance of making the right reaction to those circumstances and allowing the ultimate will of God to be reached as effectively as if he had not been ill.

My patient, the young man with the malignant lymphoma, died, but before he died his heart radiated the joy that he found in his mother's walk with the Lord. He knew that he would die but he also knew that he possessed eternal life through his belief in Christ. His funeral reflected his joy and strength as the pastor told of their visits together during his last few weeks.

Here we see that his physical condition deteriorated into death as a result of disease. But he made such a splendid response to his circumstances that he created out of it a spiritual asset in the community of much more value than most people's good health. He experienced a spiritual awakening that brought him in close cooperation with God. His reaction to evil might give rise to the fallacy that disease and suffering are the will of God. This doesn't mean that the healthy person cannot become spiritually awake but so many are spiritually asleep and not cooperating with God at all. On the other hand, so many sick people have, through their sickness, become spiritually awakened during their illness and out of the circumstances of evil they have created and set free spiritual energies far more valuable than the spiritual apathy of the healthy person.

As a Christian physician, I feel confident that the battle against disease is the will of God and I thank God for the unraveling of the mysteries of the human body and the discovery of new methods and new drugs which allow us to gain the upper hand in our fight. I also thank God for all those colleagues who are taking part in the same battle.

In the early days of our country, wolves used to descend out of the forest and do a great deal of harm. Our sturdy forefathers didn't stand around wringing their hands, talking about this being the will of God. They grabbed their guns and slaughtered the wolves. When a modern community is set upon by an invasion of germs or viruses, that is not the will of God. The situation, the problems, and the battle are the same, only the circumstances have changed.

It is a heartless act to have someone stand by the bedside of a patient and utter the pathetic complaint that disease is the will of God. I should imagine that Jesus would indignantly denounce such a thoughtless idea. When a woman with a chronic illness was brought to him, he spoke of her as "this woman . . . whom Satan hath bound, lo, these eighteen years." Jesus' attitude, both in the words he spoke and the healing miracle he so gloriously wrought, indicated his regard for disease as part of the kingdom of evil, and with all his powers he fought it and instructed his followers to do the same.

I like to think of our Lord standing by the patient's bedside, working with the doctors, nurses, and technologists in their efforts to recapture health. As the physicians minister to the body's needs, Jesus ministers to the mind and spirit in a manner that brings wholeness to the patient. If, however, the doctor's efforts fail, I like to think of Jesus showing the sufferer that, in cooperation with him, victory may still be wrested from defeat and the purposes of God realized.

It is quite natural for us to say, "Well, it's a bit careless of God to allow these things to happen if they are not his intention." It would be foolish to speak of this mystery as if all the ways of God to men were clear. I do not wish to give the impression that I can give a glib answer to specific cases of suffering that are presented to me. I, too, am often appalled at the suffering people endure, and especially little children.

Yet, in a sense, we are all like little children. Imagine a child looking into the face of his loving father and saying, "Don't you think it's mean of you to let me get hurt the way you do?" In much the same way, we look to God and say, "Look at my frustration and sorrow and disappointment and pain! How can you allow this, and how do you expect me to think you care?" Perhaps the childhood hurts are to us what our hurts are to God. He is no more callous than the ideal parent, but his perspective is different. But, the thought that comforts the child comforts me. The child, if he thought about it, might say, "There is much I don't understand but I know my father loves me and cares about what happens to me." So, for myself, I feel that because God is love there is nothing in his world than can be regarded as meaningless torture. There is much I can't understand. There must be much that I cannot be made to understand until I have passed out of the stage of childhood. But because I know God through other times and other means, and especially as revealed in Jesus, I know that although I cannot understand the answer to my question, there is an answer, and in that I can rest content.

Men came to Jesus with questions; his answers were impressive. When John the Baptist asked a question, Jesus said, "Suffer it to be so now." When Peter asked him a question, he said, "What I do thou knowest not now; but thou shalt know hereafter." And, when, on the darkest night of the world's history, the night before his death, they all asked him questions, he said, "I have yet many things to say unto you, but ye cannot bear them now."

You see, even Jesus did not say, "I have explained the world." What he did say was, "I have overcome the world," and if we can only trust where we cannot see, walking in the light we have, which is often very much like hanging on in the dark, doing faithfully that which we see to be the will of God in the circumstances which evil thrusts upon us, we can rest our minds in the assurances that circumstances which God allows, reacted to in faith and trust and courage, can never defeat purposes which God ultimately wills. So doing, we shall wrest from life something big and splendid. Our hearts will have more peace and our minds less confusion. Our labors will be done with courage and joy. And then one day—for we have been promised this—we shall look into his face and understand.

SUFFERING AND FAITH

Pain and suffering, experienced physically or mentally, can be considered from many angles but the toll it takes on faith is sometimes devastating.

Suffering is the most acute trial that faith can face; it raises the sharpest, most insistent, and most damaging questions that faith will meet. We are called upon, in suffering, to suspend judgment about unanswered questions. We must rely on a basic principle that we do not know why we suffer but we know why we trust God and he knows why we suffer. Our basic prayer is the same, "Father, I do not understand you, but I trust you." At the same time we may be asked to pay a price that is unique.

In Job, the world's classic sufferer, much of his agony was because he was racked by a critical dilemma. Was he to trust God and ask no questions or was he to display doubt as he pressed for an explanation of his predicament? At first he passed the test with honors. His fortunes were lost, his children killed, and yet his faith in God remained steadfast. "Throughout all this Job did not sin; he did not charge God with unreason" (Job 1:22, NEB). Job did not know why he was afflicted, but he knew why he trusted God and God knew why he was afflicted. In suspending judgment about his sorrow, Job revealed his faith.

But this was only the first round of his trials, and as events unfolded agony was piled on agony in seemingly endless progression. His wife encouraged him to curse God and die, his brother maintained an aloofness, his relatives quit coming, his servants ignored him, his slaves refused to acknowledge him, his children despised him, and he came to stink in the nostrils of his own family (Job 19).

Each added pressure was another layer on the dilemma. If he trusted God and suspended judgment, he had to suffer in silence. But his silence was being interpreted as guilt. He wanted to be free of guilt but he had no desire to question God's reason in reaching the answer. His faith is stretched to the breaking point and his self-defense demonstrates faith mixed with doubt.

On the one hand, Job's faith reached heights of unsurpassed courage, as when he cried, "But in my heart I know that my vindicator lives and that he will rise last to speak in court" (Job 19:25, NEB). On the other hand, his chosen style of defense led him into the bitter blackness of self-pity and doubt; understandable but wrong. God's response to this brought down even more spiritual agony as he rebuked Job, "Dare you deny that I am just or put me in the wrong that you may be right?" (Job 40:8, NEB). At the root of Job's problem lay a fallacy in this thinking (the notion that his range of information was sufficient to make proper judgments in such a situation).

Is it not the same for many of us as it was for Job? We may have no way of knowing how much strain our faith can take until we actually suffer. We should examine our anchors of faith before the day comes.

The test of suffering then reveals whether we see our suffering in view of an irreducible bedrock conviction—grounded in the revelation of God in Jesus Christ, or whether our faith is resting to any degree on what is not foundation but superstructure or just plain sand.

PRACTICAL TESTING OF FAITH

The essence of suffering is experience, not thought, and in life we see two situations where suspended judgment has practical applications. The first is when we suffer because of the injuries or hurts which come from other people.

The Christian view of life is not romantic but realistic. No one passes through life unscathed. We will all have injustices and injuries. The fabric of our lives is marked by the wear and tear of those "little torments." But each time we are injured by another's carelessness or intention we are challenged by the same questions. If we don't know why it happened, will we trust God and suspend judgment or will we demand to know why and go on to say why anyway?

Our natural tendency is "to stand up for our rights" and speak out against the wrong, and this is not altogether faulty. But it is counter productive and has little real value except to let off steam.

When suffering becomes entangled in the complex web of human relationships, we find judgment-making difficult. Some go ahead, letting the chips fall where they may. Others become introspective, searching themselves so conscientiously that they end up paralyzed by self-doubt. But if you are aware of this dilemma, you can suspend judgment and seek a shortcut through the image.

We are not primarily responsible to God for what another person does to us; he is responsible to God for that. Our responsibility to God covers our reaction to what others do to us. This is the key to our responsibility if we choose to retaliate. To forget this principle of responsibility brings resentment rather than forgiveness, reaction rather than self-control and self-pity rather than trust. Our faith is damaged by the judgments we make in such situations.

Jesus stated the principle in the Sermon on the Mount. "You have learned that they were told, 'Eye for eye, tooth for tooth.' But what I tell you is this: Do not set yourself against the man who wrongs you" (Matt. 5:38-39, NEB). This speaks directly to our thoughts when we are wrong. We suppress our own wrong, forgive the perpetrator, and forget it or retaliate in some way. To retaliate means that we have made a judgment (even if only a shallow but psychologically vital internal judgment), we have no right to make. We are then "playing God" for we have made a moral judgment as we sift through the facts and decide what to do.

Such a decision doesn't mean that we retaliate in crude or open revenge. It is more likely to produce snide remarks or secret resentment. But whatever the manner in which it expresses itself the root is the same, we have refused to suspend judgment in a situation where evil has made a mark, but the mystery of evil means we cannot judge adequately. In making judgment we have usurped God's place in judging others. So judgment is suspended and faith's part in forgiveness is experienced as we let God decide.

This theme is a constant biblical reality. Joseph forgives his brothers the grave injustice they did to him. "Am I in the place of God? You meant to do me harm; but God meant to bring good out of it" (Gen. 50:20, NEB). At the time of this meeting, Joseph had reached a position of responsibility comparable to that of a modern-day, high-level government official. He made a wise decision. He will mind his own business and leave God's business to God.

Paul makes the same point in his letter to the Romans: "Never pay back evil for evil . . . do not seek revenge, but leave a place for divine retribution; for there is a text which reads, 'Justice is mine, says the Lord, I will repay'" (Rom. 12:17-19, NEB). Or, as he writes later, "Each of us will have to answer for himself. Let us therefore cease judging one another" (Rom. 14:12-13, NEB).

Consider the mental peace, the psychological advantage of refusing to make judgments we have no right to make, then we will hold no one, neither God nor man, responsible unfairly. Instead of "an eye for an eye" we have lifted the situation to a new level where the retaliation against wrong is love and not hatred, forgiveness and not resentment, trust and not doubt. The principle of suspending judgment is thus a most important lesson in what the Book of Hebrews calls the "school of suffering" (Heb. 5:8), or in what Paul refers to as the change of heart brought by bearing "your hurt in God's way" (2 Cor. 7:10-11, NEB).

Though our responsibility to others is to forgive them as God has forgiven us, it does not mean an indulgence or softness that allows us to escape other responsibilities. Always forgiving is not the same as never punishing. I may be indulgent to my son and the result is likely to be a spoiled son, but I can be a forgiving father who disciplines his son. Forgiving judges should not mean a permissive society, a forgiving heart in a judge or a father should mean that discipline is controlled by justice and compassion, from a heart free of anger and prejudice.

What about a second type of situation, one in which there is suffering because of an injury or sickness and it is fruitless or impossible to place the blame on anyone? Both an attack of rheumatoid arthritis and a broken neck while surfing seem unjust and inexplicable. There might be small satisfaction gained from blaming someone but even this is denied to us. The situation is fundamentally demoralizing for the suffering seems meaningless.

In search of someone to answer for it, we seem to have two choices. On the one hand, we must find the answer within ourselves by resigning ourselves to it or condemming ourselves for it. On the other hand, we must answer back by accusing or at least questioning someone else. Another possible option is that God be called to the bar and charged with the injustice or all suffering which is otherwise not accountable in another way.

In placing the blame for unexplained suffering on God, we have created doubt which may change our idea of God. Our faith is lowered if our new picture of God is one in which we doubt his goodness. Then we can say, "Sure, God is responsible for my trouble." The benefit is a shelter from the heart of unanswered questions raised by apparently meaningless suffering. The harm comes from our weakened faith.

FAITH VERSUS REPRESSION

It seems that we are faced with certain pitfalls if we suspend judgment on this question. Just as we have seen the damage to faith that occurs with answering back or accusing God, we find danger in not answering back. The danger in suspending judgment is that we deny the emotional reality of our circumstance and in an unmindful way turn faith into repression.

My young patient with the malignant lymphoma did not question why he was so afflicted. (He suspended judgment.) But it would have been a completely different situation if he had denied that he had the disease. For him to raise no question was faith. For him to deny the problem would have been repression. Faith does not deny reality, rather it places it in proper perspective. To deny the presence of the enlarged lymph node whould have been the mark of make-believe, not of living faith. If this were faith, it would be clothed in evasion which condemns it to a timid, sickly existence, a pale counterfeit of true faith.

Biblical faith, in contrast, is full-blooded and down to earth. Look at Jesus' suffering and you see that to trust God did not mean for Jesus the denial of the evil and brokenness of the world but the refusal to raise the question of trusting God.

Christian attitudes toward emotions such as failure, depression, or grief have elements of unhealthy repression as expressions of present-day faith. We see this when the biblical injunction to "give thanks whatever happens" (1 Thess. 5:17, NEB) is taught with a literal interpretation. It not only contradicts much of the Bible, it can also be psychologically damaging. Yet Christians are being counseled today to praise God for evil.

Consider the possibility that this is a dangerous travesty of biblical teaching. Jesus was outraged when faced with evil; faced with sin and suffering, he wept. He did not give God thanks for everything. His anger, his tears, and his road to the cross show us how outraged God is by evil and how seriously he takes sin.

There is a dilemma here. It springs from the uncertainty between the biblical view of evil (and God hates evil) and the biblical call for faith to thank God whatever happens. This perplexing situation becomes more orderly if we think of each experience of life as a unit, and consider it in terms of its unity and its diversity.

When we are faced with a problem of life and consider it as an experience within itself, the only appropriate response to God is unquestionable trust and thanksgiving. Evil is never so great as to be irredeemable by God. From this view it is always right to trust God and give thanks.

But, at the same time, an experience of life is to be analyzed in terms of the parts that make up the puzzle. It may well be that there are elements of evil, pain, disappointment or, as the case may be, goodness, benefit, and delight. Each of these calls forth an appropriate response, and in many instances this response should not be thanks. Outrage is appropriate in response to genuine wrong, tears in response to grief, and shock in response to unexpected disaster. If you feel forced to thank God for the evil in these experiences, you will be softer on evil and harder on yourself than God is. You might think that even Christians should not give thanks for these things but it seems more logical to state that Christians especially sould not give thanks for them. Centuries ago, Augustine, as if anticipating the current teaching, wrote, "Who would wish for hardship and difficulty? You command us to endure these troubles, not to love them. No one loves what he endures even though he may be glad to endure it."

The wonder of Christian faith in time of suffering is its humanness. Where the Muslim resigns himself, the Buddhist and the Hindu withdraw, the Stoic endures, and the existentialist fights in vain, the Christian can exult. We exult because in knowing God we know the outcome, but this is no protection from the suffering of pain in between.

GOD'S ULTIMATE WILL

There is a sentence at the end of the book of Job which summarizes the message of suffering: "I know that Thou canst do all things, and that no purpose of Thine can be thwarted" (42:2, NASB). Life begins with God's intentional will when you are born again. His original plan for your well being, but your own folly and sin may spoil this plan. We then see God's circumstantial will, his will within the circumstances set up by man's evil or by the evil within the forces of nature. Finally, we see God's ultimate will, the goal he reaches, not only in spite of all man may do, but even using man's evil to further his own plan.

On the one hand, you might perceive of God's omnipotence as a means whereby he gets his own way by a sheer exhibition of his own might. On the other hand, this would make man's freedom an illusion and man's moral development would be made impossible. God's end is not imposed from without; for his end, the atonement of all souls with him must come from man's choice of God's way, not the imposition of God's will in irresistible might which leaves no room for choice. Power means ability to achieve purpose. But since the purpose is to win man's will, the use of power would defeat the purpose in that man's will would be denied. This would not be a use of power but a confession of weakness and an acceptance of defeat.

God's omnipotence, then, would not mean that nothing happens unless it is God's intention but that nothing can happen which can finally defeat him. His goal will be reached ultimately, nothing of value will be lost in the process; however, man may divert and dam up the stream of purpose nearest him, and that God—if he cannot use men as his agents—will, though with great pain to himself and to themselves, use them as his instruments.

God still controls the universe, God who also has the dreams of each of his children in mind. There is consolation in this thought about God's ultimate will. "Eye hath not seen, nor ear heard, neither have entered into the heart of man, the things which God hath prepared for them that love him" (1 Cor. 2:9). He who began the adventure of life will also control the end. "I am Alpha and Omega, the beginning and the end, the first and the last" (Rev. 22:13). The last word is with God.

10
The Doctor— God's Instrument

The practice of medicine is an art, not a trade; a calling, not a business; a calling in which your heart will be exercised equally with a head. Often the best part of your work will have nothing to do with potions and powders, but with the exercise of an influence of the strong upon the weak, of the righteous upon the wicked, of the wise upon the foolish. To you, as the trusted family counsellor, the father will come with his anxieties, the mother with her hidden grief, the daughter with her trials, and the son with his follies. Fully one third of the work you do will be entered in other books than yours. Courage and cheerfulness will not only carry you over the rough places of life, but will enable you to bring comfort and help to the weakhearted and will console you in the sad hours when, like Uncle Toby, you have "to whistle that you may not weep" (—Osler, The Master-Word in Medicine, 1903).

THE ADVANCES OF MEDICINE

When the Bible chronicled that Methuselah died at the age of 969, it set a record of longevity that is not likely to be equaled, in spite of all the advances made in recent years in the field of aging.

But the less exalted biblical goal of threescore years and ten has already been achieved in most developed countries as the average expectancy of life. Would it not be wonderful if we all were to arrive at that age in a young state and free of disease? Staying young as we grow old is largely due to what we do for ourselves, not just what medicine fails to do for us.

Our health is determined by our genetic makeup, our food, our behavior, and the nature of our environment. As societies developed into farming groups, and learned to raise crops and tame animals, nutrition improved with a consequent fall in the death rate of children and an explosion of the population. This expansion was periodically checked by crop failures, famine, tribal wars, and infectious diseases.

Steadily increasing food supplies stimulated increased birthrates and resistance to infectious diseases. A massive population growth followed. The world population grew at a rapid rate to 750 million by 1750, to one billion by 1830, to two billion by 1930, to three billion by 1960, and now to four billion people.

A continuous flow of improvements in the field of agriculture began in the eighteenth century with increased land use. The fields were fertilized and restored with manure; crop rotation was practiced; and potatoes and maize became widely cultivated. Mechanization was begun during the industrial revolution of the nineteenth and twentieth centuries. This was quickly followed by irrigation practices, chemical fertilization, and pesticides. The past thirty years has been a virtual "Green Revolution" with further increased food production. This was based primarily on genetic manipulations which produced hardier and more productive varieties of crops, responsive to the more intensive use of water and fertilizer.

It is thought that more than half the reduction in death rates over the past three centuries occurred before 1900 and was due in nearly equal measure to improved nutrition and reduced exposure to air and waterborne infection. The decrease in deaths caused by infection was due in large measure to: (1) safer water and milk supplies; (2) the improvement in both personal and food hygiene; and (3) the efficient disposal of sewage.

In 1796, Edward Jenner vaccinated James Phipps, an English lad, with fluid from a cowpox blister on the arm of Sarah Nelmes, a milkmaid. Two months later Jenner tested James with fluid from the blister of a patient with smallpox, and smallpox did not develop. This successful test marked the beginning of vaccinations against specific infectious diseases. Deaths from smallpox began to fall in the nineteenth century to be followed by decrease in deaths from diphtheria, whooping cough, lock-jaw, polio, measles, and tuberculosis in the twentieth century.

When we look at the factors leading to the likelihood of a long and fruitful life, the two with greatest impact were the improvement in nutrition and reduction of infection through improved sanitation. Vaccination against specific infectious diseases has contributed to a smaller degree. An even smaller contribution has been made by the introduction of medical and surgical therapy of modern medicine in the twentieth century. This has led the critics of modern medicine to emphasize the failures of medicine while overlooking the advances. Claims are made that we spend a great deal of money for health care but the life expectancy curve stays about level. This fails to take into account the relief of the handicap's pain and fear that are a part of many diseases and can drastically change the enjoyment of life, but are not shown in the statistics of death and disability. It leaves an unclear, incomplete picture.

No practical science affects our lives as directly and personally as medicine. A world without nuclear power would not be too difficult to conceive; but where would we be without penicillin? The medical advances of the past century have erased some of the fear of living under the constant threat of diseases that were poorly understood and ineffectively remedied 100 years ago.

The knowledge gap between the physicians of 1877 and today's doctors is as great as the gap between the aviation knowledge of the Wright Brothers and Neil Armstrong. The ruggedness of medicine as a profession, when the physician had to rely on ingenuity, persuasion, luck, improvisation, and prayer to overcome the great technical obstacles he faced, is remembered in many parts of our country even today.

My father died of pneumonia in a cabin in the mountains of North Carolina in 1930. I have been told of the trips made on horseback by Dr. Locke Robinson, a legendary figure, to ease his pain. There was little else he could do; but his efforts were viewed, at that time and in that place, with awe and appreciation. His doctor's bag contained few effective tools. Digitalis was used to treat heart failure, and pain was lessened with opium. For most disorders he could provide a variety of useless potions and salves that were administered in desperation and blind faith. The stethoscope and the reflex hammer were his major diagnostic instruments. One can imagine the awe with which that doctor would view today's sophisticated tools for visual diagnosis. What would he think of the computerized radio-scaning techniques that can locate tiny areas of damaged tissue in inaccessible organs like the pancreas and brain and can display those tissues on a television screen? What would he think of using a flexible, lighted, fiber-optic tube to look directly at an ulcer in the patient's stomach, search for a site of bleeding, or examine a small lung tumor?

Medical knowledge, like other scientific knowledge, is accumulated at an ever-accelerating rate; and revolutionary changes in the diagnosis and treatment of disease have taken place within the professional lifetime of most doctors practicing today. It is commonplace for a doctor to order an analysis of the many components of the blood on a hospitalized or ambulatory patient today, although the analysis of substances in the blood did not become a major method of diagnosis until around the time of World War II. Even twenty years ago, no one could have imagined the automatic equipment now used to study blood samples. In a very short time, this equipment measures the levels of enzymes, minerals, and waste products in the blood and indicates which of these fall outside the normal healthy range. Further sophistication of these machines will allow them to be programmed to give different possible diagnoses based on blood sample data, indicate the probability of each diagnosis, and request further information from the physician.

In the past few years, an ever-increasing parade of all sorts of devices have passed from hypothesis to reality in solving the problems of faulty function of various parts of the body. Synthetic parts such as heart valves, blood vessels, hips, knee joints, and teeth can all be used to replace their natural counterparts when they falter or malfunction. For diseases such as diabetes the search continues for a workable mechanical gland to supply insulin as the body needs it. Electronic pacemakers keep the heart beating regularly, and people who suffer kidney failure can live their lives, although restricted, with the aid of a dialysis machine. Surgeons now are performing operations long thought to be technically impossible. The heart-lung machine has made possible open-heart surgery; laser beams are used to correct abnormalities in the lining of the back of the eyeball, and organ transplants are no longer in the realm of science fiction.

We have seen many new drugs approved for use against different diseases. This represents an incredible advance in the chemical approach to disease with a radical change in those drugs in use today from those prescribed just a decade ago. With the important exceptions of aspirin, insulin, digitalis, and a few other standbys, the doctor's list of effective drugs has changed completely since the 1950s. These advances in the drug therapy have been intimately connected to progress in our theoretical understanding of life processes at the cellular and molecular levels.

The study of life at the cellular level is a young and fast-growing part of medicine. Virtually all of modern biochemistry stems from the discovery of the structure of DNA, the materials which codes the body's genetic information. Continuing work has shown that researchers now have the theoretical tools to begin answering questions that could have been raised but not solved before. Modern biochemical research brings closer the possibility of solution of the deadly mystery of cancer. Cancer cells are characterized chiefly by their ability to multiply almost indefinitely, gradually taking over larger and larger areas of the body. Understanding of the disease process is gradually being gained, as scientists study the very basic biochemical processes that control normal cell division; how we grow, how cuts heal, and how new blood cells are made day by day.

Medical knowledge accumulates too fast to allow anyone to learn and assimilate all the recent discoveries and technological changes in any field of medicine. Medicine has become increasingly specialized and even this narrowing of a field of interest doesn't assure that a doctor will stay well informed even of advances in his own chosen field. If doctors find it hard to understand all of modern medicine, consider how lost a layman, without special training, would feel in trying to penetrate the air of mystification surrounding the field of medical research. Physicians need to improve their communication to patients. The language needs to be understandable and thorough. This would help stem the tide of malpractice suits and promote understanding of our work.

THE NATURE OF DISEASE

Science has perfected many new tools to unravel the secrets of man's innermost being. Most of this has improved our ability to be accurate in the diagnosis of disease, but it has unfortunately emphasized the importance of the biochemistry of the body while neglecting the natural history of the disease. Even in the day of advanced technology there are many diseases, especially chronic disorders, which are not curable or reversible. It is essential that we learn the natural history of diseases, how they begin, how they develop their phases of improving and worsening, and their final consequences. Biochemistry can't teach this. It is learned only at the exam table, or bedside, by studying as many examples of as many diseases as possible. Each example may have unique features for it involves a different patient.

Doctors search out the secrets of life, continually improving their ability to recognize and interpret the factors that affect use for better or worse. All persons are different and competent doctors recognize the great importance of this. Two people can change from good health to sickness to recovery, each at a different rate, even when the disease is the same. Some of us may be distressed by the problems of life while others are stable—these differences account for some of the variation of the effects of sickness.

From a physical point of view, there are vast differences among us. Physical differences are vast, mental variations are probably even greater. Each of us has a different nervous system and different life experiences. Our mental activity is so complex that only a few manifestations are capable of being classified or categorized. When behavior is abnormal, it is usually diagnosed by giving it a particular term or phrase. Deciding that the behavior is abnormal is difficult enough; trying to give it a name has proved to be futile in many instances. This is known by astute physicians who will handle their patients in accord with what has been learned from watching a patient's reaction pattern. Physicians who don't notice such patterns may blame their patients for odd behavior and be surprised because their treatments get poor results.

THE PHYSICIAN'S ROLE

The vastness of the possible mental and physical variations in people complicates the doctor's task when he is trying to work through the symptoms of a patient. The doctor's concern is for the

THE DOCTOR—GOD'S INSTRUMENT

patient and the patient places his hope in the doctor. Even with contributions from nurses, laboratory and X-ray technologists, pharmacists, social workers, and others, the relationship is most strong between these two—the sick and the healer. The doctor, in a different way, may also have to minister to the patient's spouse, father, mother, brothers, sisters, neighbors, and employer, for they are all interested in the patient's sickness. The doctor is constantly striving for two goals: (1) the preservation of life; and (2) the prevention or relief of suffering. He preserves life by treating illness and this presumes that he has uncovered the story of the sickness, visualized the past for clues to this illness, and has an idea of how things will go in the near future. He must search for details in the life of the patient that will lead him to an accurate diagnosis—effective treatment requires this. Both patient and doctor are helped by this collection of information. The patient's illness becomes clearer and the doctor's understanding of human nature and disease is broadened.

Medicine is learned principally from patients. Medical students learn by observing and to some extent, participating in the relationship between an experienced doctor and his patient. Medical information is vast but not infinite. Much material, but not all, may be read and remembered well enough to be useful when added to practical experience. Medical skill is a combination of these.

As a physician considers his patients' problems, he responds to sensory cues of which he is unaware. He considers the evidence of the case—what does it point to? He must have a background of knowledge about many different disease patterns and he compares the symptoms with the likely possibilities. Finally, he reasons the problem in his mind, tossing out certain diagnoses, retaining others, raising new questions, deciding what further testing to do, considering all the options at hand.

A doctor becomes a better doctor by increasing his store of knowledge; he does this by talking to and examining large numbers of patients. All the while he is using the store of knowledge in treating each new patient; so he not only increases in knowledge but in wisdom. If he has a large, excessively busy practice, he may not be able to spend enough time with each patient to acquire such a store of knowledge. On the other hand, his practice may be too small to allow him to see as many examples of different diseases to serve this purpose. He as well as all other doctors, can supplement this type of practice by attending conferences and lectures.

Within two to three minutes after beginning to talk with a patient, the doctor starts to formulate a hypothesis. Doctors can't work without hypotheses. For every new patient the doctor will create one or more hypotheses. It is more accurate to ask a doctor what his hypothesis is rather than what the diagnosis is when a particular problem is confronted. A hypothesis may be the same as a diagnosis but generally is a working diagnosis and treatment plan. The passage of time will prove or disprove the correctness of hypothesis. If it is correct, it become the diagnosis; if incorrect, it is discarded. In either case, it has served its temporary purpose of organizing and directing the doctor's thoughts as he diagnoses the patient's illness. Hypotheses require skepticism by the doctor. They may melt away into nothing, either by the course of the patient's illness or by new information which points to a specific disease. A physician who never doubts his diagnosis may be too busy or unwilling to consider the reality of what is going on. When a well-informed doctor is confronted by a complicated or unusual problem, he takes the time to reflect and automatically turns the problem over in his mind until he finds the best solution for that particular time.

Though the doctor has doubts and though the patient senses these, the doctor must develop the art of communicating the news to the patient in a way that will, if possible, strengthen the patient's hope and confidence. The physician who recognizes this as the nature of the practice of medicine will be a more honest and effective doctor than one who hides his doubts or denies that he has any. It is not doubt but its misuse that is harmful.

The doctor not only creates hypotheses, makes diagnoses, and prescribes treatments, but he is also a dispenser of hope. The fear and concerns surrounding the diagnosis of disease requires treatment just as surely as does the disease. The doctor may do this by frequent brief reports regarding the patient's condition and what is to be expected from the treatment. His appearance and attitude of confidence, suggesting that he understands and is in control of the situation, does a great deal toward soothing troubled minds. Successful treatment depends greatly on preserving, restoring, or strengthening the patient's hope. Anxiety is relieved, anticipation is less fearful, symptoms are lessened, therapy is more effective.

The pastor joins the doctor in generating and preserving hope. The doctor does so in reference to the medical situation. In the past, the appearance of the pastor was frequently the same as announcing to the family that the end was near. The pastor's role today is more appreciated for the hope of eternal life that is in Christ, and for the concern he shows for the patient. The doctor's activities with respect to hope may overlap those of the pastor if the physician in charge is of strong faith. In this instance, he may be as able as the pastor in pointing the way to eternal life.

The doctor with a strong faith will confidently impress upon his patient the need to examine his life for a spiritual void. Hope cannot be delivered on a platter of superficial actions such as pats on the shoulder or expressions such as, "Keep up the good work." It must have the power to defeat doubt. The Christian physician can encourage by suggesting prayer and appropriate Bible verses and by reaffirming the claims of faith. The Christian doctor, however, must be certain to maintain his clinical skills at a high level—he cannot hide sloppy work behind a facade of religiousness.

Usually a physician generates or preserves hope by stating a specific treatment plan and adhering to it until he considers it wise to change. He does not encourage hope by persuading a patient to cheerfulness where that person faces a life of severe discomfort, lessened productivity, and a lack of joy because of a disability. The physician shows that he believes he is able to help the patient by having specific plans. If, in addition, the doctor demonstrates that he studies the patient's medical problems over and over, he strengthens the patient's hope that however difficult the problem, it may still be solved. The physician is helped in reaching sound clinical decisions by listening to the patient's story of his symptoms, and the patient is reassured that the physician is interested in helping him. On the other hand, if the physician doesn't take the time to plan and institute a detailed therapeutic program, the patient who is slowly improving or is not improving at all, is justified in concluding that his situation is hopeless and that he is doomed to suffer. Such a physician has a low standing as a healer.

It is important that one of the goals of a treatment program be the relief of pain and suffering. If the patient doesn't get better, the situation must be studied in light of the patient's condition at that time and a different treatment begun. Day by day, physicians turn over and over in their minds the questions of a patient's condition, even though the patient visited the doctor days earlier.

THE HEALING CHRIST

Dr. Jack W. Provonsha, writing in the *Current Medical Digest* for December 1959, spoke of Jesus as the model for modern medicine.

It has become traditional to identify modern doctors in spirit with a long line of historic greats reaching back to the impressive Hippocrates. This notable Greek, a veritable pinnacle in ancient medicine, often called the "Father of Medicine," largely set the pattern for current professional attitudes and relationships. But sometimes it is forgotten that medicine owes its greatest debt not to Hippocrates, but to Jesus. It was the humble Galilean who more than any other figure in history bequeathed to the healing arts their essential meaning and spirit. During this Christmas season physicians would do well to remind themselves that without His spirit, medicine degenerates into depersonalized methodology, and its ethical code becomes a mere legal system. Jesus brings to methods and codes the corrective of love without which true healing is rarely actually possible. The spiritual "Father of Medicine" was not Hippocrates of the island of Cos, but Jesus of the town of Nazareth!

THE CHRISTIAN AS A DOCTOR

The Christian physician will look at the events of life in a way that his work will be interpreted as truly a vocation from God. His interpretation will be reaffirmed each time he enters the hospital or office. If his vocation is a means of achieving great financial rewards or social status in society, he is missing the heart of the meaning of his work. Doctors usually have a high social standing and a comfortable living but there can be no Christian vocation if the job is undertaken as a way of enriching the self, rather than serving the patient.

The Christian doctrine of creation places man in a position to share dominion over God's world. The engineer exercises dominion in one area, the doctor in another. From the time of Jesus, the Christian faith has regarded the body as worthy of healing. It is not to be shunned, in favor of the saving of the soul, but healed. The healed body, then, is to be used in gratitude for the benefit of man and the glory of God.

Healing of the physically ill body requires knowledge of the body's workings. Interest in biology and concern for the technical knowledge of the body's physiology are primary ingredients in the doctor's work. Man is not a soul without a body and he is not a body without a mind or spirit. The doctor's interest and training must allow him to do more than tinker with a mechanism. He must heal a whole person. His work carries him into the lives of people in their most profound moments. In birth and death, he is likely to be with the family before anyone else, even the pastor.

The doctor must want to help people; not because he knows that it would be nice to do so, but because that is the way the job gets done in the best fashion. The doctor's work is with particular patients with particular problems and for these patients, he meets crises with whatever he has available at that time. If this has no meaning for the Christian doctor, his work can hardly be a Christian vocation. The Bible relates God's work in history with tough problems throughout their life's history. This should furnish meaning for the Christian practicing medicine.

The doctor, as a practitioner, must attain a high degree of technical skill and competence. The healing of pneumonia will occur from the penicillin ordered by the morally responsible non-Christian physician. There is not Christian penicillin. To suggest that a Christian doctor has special resources for healing or for making diagnoses is both foolish and wrong. The practice of medicine may have a different meaning for the Christian but the job remains rooted in the same biological and human realities and competence is measured in human judgment.

For the Christian doctor there are temptations to drag religion into his practice on a pious level. For example, when a patient dies and the doctor fulfills his duty to inform the family, it is not his obligation to deliver a funeral oration or to become preachy. The family can expect the news to be brought in a poised, sympathetic way. Any doctor will know that death is a very traumatic experience which grieves those who survive, and he will show sympathy. A Christian doctor will also know that death is not an ultimate tragedy, and he will not be overwhelmed. He will show his acceptance of death as a natural inevitability and as a creative episode in the pilgrimage of all men.

The doctor must act with authenticity in his encounter with patients and their families. Kindness and confidence mark his entry, not gushing or loudness. His professional sureness isn't overbearing. He feels concern and empathy for his patients but his involvement doesn't cause a loss of poise or proportion. It is likely that he will be remembered by his patients for what he stands for in the broad commitments of his life rather than what he said at the time of their crisis.

The doctor's witness will be shown if he is a dedicated friend who practices medicine in a sensitive, sensible and fruitful way and is a loyal and faithful church member. His interest in Christian thought and living along with the adequacy and thoroughness of his professional services become witnesses to his faith. The main expression of medicine as a Christian vocation is in skillful performance. The real difference to the doctor is the meaning it has for him—that this is God's will for his life.

11
A Blueprint for Change

A PROSPECTIVE VIEW OF HEALTH

For years I have tried different methods, some good, some not so good, to bring patients to a new understanding of health. It is sad to see Mr. Allen, for example, a thirty-six-year-old man, crippled by nonactivity due to coronary heart disease. His attacks of chest pain are frequent, forcing his family to plan their lives around his need for medical care.

This picture of limited activity due to chronic disease is repeated in 25 percent of the people in the 45-69 age groups; people who should be in their most productive years. I have had many patients express the wish that they could have known what to do to prevent becoming chronically ill. They look at their health retrospectively; after the fact.

Many of these chronically ill patients will have a course like Mr. Campbell. He began having chest pain at age forty-two, four years before his death from a heart attack. During these four years, his blood pressure was not well controlled and he suffered a mild stroke. These two vascular diseases will account for over 50 percent of all deaths of Americans each year.

There is another view of health; the prospective view. This is an outlook characterized by foresight. Health is expected to be good because the right habits are followed. Good health is a planned part of life; attained through a progression of analysis setting goals, implementing and evaluating a plan to reach those goals. The doctor wants to reduce your risks of disease to zero or to return you to this point if you are sick. You are, however, not achieving your goal of good health at this point. You are at the point of stable health, far less healthy than you can become. To advance from a point of stable health with no known risks to total wholeness requires a creative approach to the problem. It is a worthwhile goal; all of life is lived more abundantly if you are healthy and have a proper balance of life.

THE FAMILY—A LOGICAL BEGINNING

In the past the family served as one means to protect its members. The family is the logical unit to begin building or rebuilding habits and changing behavior. In time, family members, by encouragement and by learning together, can experience the pleasure of once again protecting its members. In this way each becomes more conscious of the stages of the process and becomes more accurate in his predictions of what to do next. Each one becomes more skillful at choosing a better way to move forward; developing a consciousness of the process of change and determining the method that is likely to work best. Here are a few more keys to creativity.

1. Freedom from false pride
2. Belief in your ability to succeed
3. Constructive discontent
4. Ability to control habits

KEYS TO CREATIVE BEHAVIOR

Families can become more creative in their life-style by simply becoming more conscious of what they do and how what they do relates to their internal and external environment. If, for example, several family members are overweight, this is usually a result of eating too much. Families can recall how much more attractive clothes looked, how much more quickly they moved, and how much more energy they had when they were slimmer. Each can recreate the sequence of events that marked the change from slimness to fatness. Next, each can gauge what is yet to come if changes aren't made.

FREEDOM FROM FALSE PRIDE

Self-discipline (consistently behaving the best way) is another way to say "Freedom from false pride." The tendency to "hold your head up high" may spell doom to your efforts toward change. Such an attitude may stifle curiosity and keep you from asking the key questions. It restricts a change of mind or direction which thereby fixes a preconceived and prejudicial course. False pride joins the other six "deadly sins"—greed, lust, sloth, envy, gluttony, and hate—and diverts our attention from improvement. It is too much "How great I am" and not enough "What changes do I need to make?"

On the other hand, self-discipline is behaving in the light of truth and reality. It requires the courage of convictions and the fearless acceptance of the responsibility of being what we are, knowing what we know and do not know and of taking the steps required to insure our own development. We are, then, encouraged to even enlarge our knowledge, increase sensitivity, and form a true philosophy of freedom.

BELIEF IN YOUR ABILITY TO SUCCEED

Feeling strongly that you can succeed is not the same as being egotistical or a braggart. It is simply a necessary trait for the further development of your creative behavior. It is right to encourage yourself. If you wait for someone else to supply the encouragement, you may find yourself headed in an uncomfortable direction.

You may fail to develop your traits through the mistaken idea that you are more socially acceptable and attractive if you remain "humble." Gentleness toward others is not to be mistaken for weakness. The stronger the belief in your own abilities the easier it is for you to forego your privileges for the rights of others. Believe in your own creative potential and you are creative.

CONSTRUCTIVE DISCONTENT

Becoming an adolescent usually generates discontent. It seems to go with that period of life. Nothing is right, everything needs improvement. Having the attitude of discontent is not enough, the end result is often a "bunch of gripes."

As we age, our discontent weakens; we may find it easier to accept the status quo of the normal, average person. We may feel that we "have it made" and are content to lie on beds of ease. This is a destructive attitude. Just as we attain the wisdom of experience we yield our lean and hungry attitudes in search of the good life. A constructive attitude is necessary for dynamic people; discontent is demanded for problem solving. Combined discontent and constructive attitude define a quality that marks the person who can approach problems, without fear, for he knows that something better will be the final result.

Bad habits may be designated "bad" because this is the way we "feel" about them. We may learn through a book, the newspaper, television, or from some other knowledgeable source that, in fact, a certain habit is harmful to our health. If we combine the way we feel with what we know, we bring our behavior into a more balanced whole. If we sense that something is wrong, gain the knowledge of what is wrong and then decide to correct it, we are more in control of our potential.

ABILITY TO CONTROL HABITS

From the beginning of life you learn and you commit that learning to your memory. Afterwards you tend to behave in ways which reflect your learning. Both good habits and bad habits are a part of what you have learned. A habit is preconceived behavior and, if bad, will hinder your health, your dreams, and your desires. Each of us often acts by intuition, this being a part of the pattern of preconceived behavior. Intuition is valuable but it tends to retard creative behavior if you allow yourself to be locked into a preconceived approach to life. To be able to see things in different ways, it is absolutely necessary to be in control of your habit—always ready to discard a way of doing things if your development is hindered.

Steady development in a creative way, then, requires a steady, determined effort. Desirable behavior patterns can be learned. This is the only way to obtain them. They are not a quirk of birth nor are they magic. Creativity in changing a life-style of bad habits demands listening to your own logical and sensitive conclusions, not to the dictates of the immediate environment, society, friends, or acquaintances.

BLOCKS TO CREATIVITY

There are many opportunities to be wrong. Some mistakes carry stiffer penalties than others. Still your fear of being wrong delays

A BLUEPRINT FOR CHANGE

action; most of the time you may seem to be waiting until you know it all, until you are declared an "expert" before you can speak up or act up to a situation. Yet you don't become an "expert" and you are kept from change by your own pride, fear, jealousy, and competiveness. You may block your own creativity by the following.

Fear of making mistakes
Fear of being seen as a fool
Fear of criticism
Fear of being misused
Fear of being alone
Fear of disturbing tradition
Fear of losing the security of habit
Fear of losing the love of the group
Fear of truly being an individual

Being afraid of change is natural and normal. Fear is, however, often greatly lessened through your determination to deal with the unexpected through knowledge and preparation. Fear restrains you and misdirects your energy and action. You overcome fear by changing your focus from "I don't want to be wrong" to "I will try to be right."

DESIGN FOR CHANGING A LIFE-STYLE

Everyone is a problem-solver. Teachers, farmers, writers, secretaries, and plumbers are all problem-solvers. Some do it better than others. People who behave creatively relative to problem situations and generate uniquely satisfying solutions are those who understand the process of change through a design of a new situation.

The process of design describes a series of phases through which the journey of change must pass. These include your intentions, your decisions, your actions, and your evaluations. There are seven such phases and they follow a logical sequence:

Accept situation	to find the reasons for changing a habit
Assess or analyze	to get the facts and feelings, the ins and outs of the problem
Define	to determine the essential goals concerning the problem situation
Ideate	to generate options for achieving the essential goals, to search out all the ways of getting to the major goals

Select   to choose from the options;
                     determine the best way to go
Implement   to take action or plan to act
Evaluate   review progress and plan again

By now you recognize that this is a multistage experience. There are several different techniques for advancing through each of these phases. You will find that the best technique is the one which works best for you. This may involve simply "taking a chance" or "writing it down." This method is designed to prevent your becoming an "impossible dreamer." Avoid the trap of prejudice. Prejudice means prejudging; knowing the answer before you begin. Try to defer judgment until all the facts are known.

PHASE I
Acceptance

Let's assume that you are displeased with the image facing you as you stand before a mirror. Your muscles sag because they are too soft, and the layer of fat covering them is too thick. Your breathing gets short when you walk up a flight of steps. Your energy runs out before the day is over. These are some of the indications that your physical condition needs improving.

Healthy feelings and emotions play a significant role in your work, your family relationships, and in your general health. If you have feelings of resentment toward your spouse, your children, your friends, or your fellow employees you need to evaluate the basic cause of these feelings. If you have difficulty making and maintaining close friendships, you need to look at your ability to love.

If your life revolves around a schedule of work, eat, sleep, and evening television, without a time for contemplation of your relationship to God, you need to consider a change in your schedule. Time, skills, money, and experience may be used wisely and still not be in complete balance because they have not been used to build eternal values. At this point you should be aware if you have a problem. The next step is to accept the problem in a creative fashion.

To accept a problem means to assume responsibility for it—an act of self-giving. Diving into a problem with the "best of intentions" without careful consideration of the time and interest required may

A BLUEPRINT FOR CHANGE

end in frustrated failure. It is always more difficult to back out of a problem after committing yourself to its resolution than it is to reject participation from the outset.

Acceptance is the first major step in solving any problem. Deeper learning, greater satisfaction, and greater pleasure can only be achieved if the acceptance of the situation in question is wholehearted. This will take a dedication of time and energy and perhaps a change in your list of priorities.

The way you accept a problem will have value in determining the outcome of your efforts. Generally you get out of something in proportion to what you put into it, that is your mood or emotional frame usually determines your level of enjoyment. For example, you may wish to lose two pounds of weight this week. Your interest in doing this will depend on how important it is for you to begin the journey to creative change within your own life. Your success will be greatly enhanced if you have a clear idea of the demands of the problem as measured in money, time, stress, and so forth, and the existing demands are not in conflict or can be altered or eliminated.

WHO'S IN CHARGE?

The decision of acceptance involves two profound choices in life: to accept things as they exist or to accept the responsibility for changing them. Recognition of a situation which controls your life needlessly is the path to choosing to live with that control or to accept the task of removing it as a control over your life.

Acceptance, therefore, can be encouraged by constantly reminding yourself of "who's in charge" of your life and realizing that freedom and self-control are yours only if you accept the responsibility to change your life by removing the needless situation.

WHAT'S HOLDING YOU BACK?

There are three main causes for not accepting the challenge and change a life-style. In the first place, it seems likely to be, or actually will be, mentally or physically punishing to do it. Secondly, the importance of doing it is not understood. Thirdly, there are other problems which come before or stand in the way.

All of these can be overcome, but it is first necessary to identify which of them will apply. Then it becomes a matter of giving yourself the authority to control your behavior in a conscious way. You analyze what you do and ask yourself why you do it. Finally you find a way to reward or punish yourself for desirable or undesirable behavior.

BREAKING HABITS

Since acceptance calls for adaptation to new situations, the barriers between you and accepting your problem are your habits. You don't want to change from what you are doing and you resist being "told" to do so by the problem. After you have assessed your long-range goals and have decided that the problem does fit into your life, you then have to break those habits which prevent your acceptance of the problem and painstakingly form a set of new ones. It will help to make a list of the reasons you don't want to face the problem or why you are afraid to face the problem. The list may well include those habits which make your current life-style comfortable. Next take each item and replace it with new accepting behavior. It will not be easy but the difficulty will be repaid by the excitement of opening new doors into your problem for you to enter it more easily.

PHASE II
The Assessment or Analysis

You began this phase in chapter 10 as you clarified what you already knew and gathered new information about fitness, mental health, spiritual health, and behavior.

To analyze behavior or life-style means: to take the problems apart; to research and question the subject; to discover interrelationships and patterns; to examine parts in relation to the whole; to gather facts and opinions; to spread the problem out before yourself.

INTERRELATIONSHIPS—LIFE-STYLE AND DISEASE

Cigarette smoking, alcoholism, and obesity are a combination of harmful behavior and sickness. These are tough medical problems without simple solutions. Many people smoke cigarettes until emphysematous, overeat until obese, and drink alcohol until cirrhotic, in spite of knowing better. These three habits are hard to

A BLUEPRINT FOR CHANGE

crack; each causes undesirable changes in body functions that affect health. We are unable to adapt to the dangers they impose.

Obesity is, in part, a result of adaptation; stemming from the time when human societies lived under unpredictable conditions with frequent food scarcity. Occasionally food was abundant; stimulating overeating. Now we have abundant food; the same urge that once saved our lives now threatens to endanger our survival by making us obese.

Cigarette smoking and alcohol drinking, on the other hand, are not done in response to a basic need of the body. Once begun for whatever reason, they become a complex mixture of addiction to the alcohol or nicotine, a daily ritual, a response to social influences, a release of boredom or a relief of stress. Just as overeating fills psychological needs, so do alcohol and nicotine. Unfortunately, the body cannot adapt to the harmful effects of obesity or to the pollutants in cigarette smoke or to the alcohol in wines, beers, or whiskeys. Most smokers get chronic bronchitis or emphysema and many smokers get cancer of the lung. Many alcohol drinkers get cirrhosis of the liver and many overeaters get obesity. Each of these habits represents undesirable behavior. Until we are convinced of the need of change, the assessment is not complete.

PHASE III
Definition

At this stage of designing a change of life-style we need to bridge the gap between the analyzed facts just discovered and the consideration of alternatives that will follow. Definition is a refinement of the "real problem." One person might define his life-style in terms that state his current understanding of the problem. Another person might define it as the truth as far as it is known at this time. Such comments indicate the need to ask the question, "What is the real problem?" The response must be clear, complete, and meaningful. If a meaningful definition isn't expressed, it could mean that the analysis has been too superficial.

PROBLEMS WITHIN PROBLEMS

Inside each problem caused by a behavior or habit there are many related subsituations. Locating and resolving the key subproblems that generate the whole situation is another way of defining the job that is to be done. For example, Mr. Pender smokes cigarettes and weighs too much. His blood pressure is too high and his cholesterol level is 278 mgs. There is a relationship between his overeating, his high cholesterol, and his blood pressure. He needs to search further. Is he overeating as a result of family teachings and traditions; does he have bad habits at coffee-break time; does he stop at the tavern for a beer or two with friends after work? Finally, how firm is his will to change, his incentive, his motivation to control his excessive eating and to bridle his smoking habit?

Many Americans have unhealthy lives due to unhealthy habits and most know it. There is a reluctance to begin a change in lifestyle, choosing rather to follow a life of pleasure and comfort. Many other people, however, believe it wise to change their habits if their health will improve.

Three major reasons have been identified for eating less. Appearance is the number one reason; the fact that clothes don't fit is the number two reason; and doctor's orders is number three. Lack of success in dieting is usually due to a lack of willpower and discipline.

The three top reasons for exercising are to feel better, to stay healthy, and to lose weight. Lack of time, lack of discipline, and poor health are three reasons for not exercising.

The three top reasons for stopping smoking are to improve health, to please children or other family members, and because the doctor recommended it. The three top reasons for continuing to smoke are it's a habit hard to break, it's enjoyable, and it relaxes and calms nerves.

PHASE IV
Ideation

Searching for ideas is the next stage in the process of designing a new life-style. You have defined your directions and your goal is clearly described. It is time now to generate options, alternative ways to achieve your goal.

BRAINSTORMING

If you want ideas, you've got to ask the questions which beg for ideas. "What can I do about eating too much?" is such a question.

A BLUEPRINT FOR CHANGE

"How can I quit smoking?" or "how can I start an exercise program?" are others.

Brainstorming these basic questions with a small group of three or four persons, possibly other family members, will generate scores of ideas for each of these problems in a very short time. An analysis of eating behavior for example would generate ideas. The following statements, if they seem appropriate to your life-style, could be used:

> I eat too fast at meals.
> Snacking between meals is a part of my daily schedule.
> Eating is not particularly enjoyable to me.
> I would rather fix food that is processed than take more time with my cooking.
> I am not careful about the proper balance of my food.
> Desserts are a daily part of my food intake.
> I rarely give thought to balancing my food intake with my physical activity.
> My appetite is usually satisfied before I feel too full.
> Very often I grab and eat snack meals standing up.

The same type of statement analysis can be useful in generating ideas to quit smoking or initiate an exercise program. The originator of brainstorming, Alex Osborn, lays down four requirements for all who participate in a session. Anyone can learn to apply them. The brainstorming session is automatically retarded when the rules are ignored. The four requirements are:

> Defer judgment. (Criticize later if necessary.)
> Freewheel your ideas.
> Tag on. (Make another idea out of the last one given by changing it.)
> Strive for large numbers. (Don't hold back for a minute.)

Each brainstorming session should last about five minutes per subject and extend no longer than fifteen to twenty minutes.

PHASE V
Selection of Ideas

Now that you know what it is you want to do (definition) and have considered and collected many alternate ways for getting there, the next step is to select one or more of those "ways" from the many. It is time to decide which idea fulfills the requirements of your objectives better than all the others . . . decision-making time.

You, for example, may want to stop smoking because of the widespread publicity about the dangers of cigarette smoking or because of pressure from your family. You may be aware of the numerous antismoking, drugs, devices, educational programs, and group methods that have been promoted to the public.

These include the following methods:

Fear—The traditional method of encouraging people to stop smoking has been to frighten these by elaborating on the possible consequences. This approach can backfire, however, because some patients will smoke more to relieve their anxiety, and others become so defensive that they only strengthen their resolve to keep smoking.

Drugs—Many drugs have been tried as substitutes for tobacco. These include lobeline (Indian tobacco), Bantron, Niloban; a nicotine containing chewing gum used in Sweden; and valium, equanil, or other antianxiety drugs. None of these have been effective in reducing smoking.

Filters—Several types of filters are on the market, including the heavily promoted "One Step at a Time: by Teledyne Water Pik, which costs about $10.00 and includes four filters, each to be used for two weeks to gradually eliminate about 90% of the tar, nicotine, and carbon monoxide. The success of this method can perhaps be measured by the separate availability of filter number four (two for $5.00), for those who do not quit smoking at the end of eight weeks.

Aversive Conditioning—Deter, a drug claimed to make tobacco smoke taste unpleasant, electric shock, blowing smoke at the smoker, and rapid smoking are aversive methods designed to make smoking unpleasant. Some patients using the rapid smoking method, inhaling smoke every six seconds until dizzy or nauseated, have developed abnormal electrocardiograms or rapid heart rates.

Clinics and Organized Groups—Clinics and organized groups may help some smokers stop, at least temporarily. Some studies have indicated long-term success rates of about 20 to 25 percent. Many organized groups plans are available; their elaborateness, and possibly even their expensiveness, may contribute to their effectiveness. The Seventh-Day Adventists sponsor a Five-Day Plan, which offers lectures by physicians and clergymen, explanations or smoking cessation techniques, and group meetings. Schick Laboratories in California has a program for one hour on five consecutive days that relies mainly on aversion therapy, including rapid smoking and electrical shocks, followed by eight weeks of reinforcement in weekly one-hour sessions; this program costs about $500.00. Smok-Enders offer eight weekly meetings with a highly structured program emphasizing self-awareness, behavior modification, positive conditioning, and periodic reunions for a year afterward. The Smok-Enders Program costs from $225 to $295 in various parts of the country.

Self-Help Methods—A number of antismoking programs recommend various types of rituals and record keeping. One method is to smoke only at set times during the day, regardless of location or activity; if the allotted time occurs when the smoker is unable to smoke, that particular cigarette is omitted. Another method is to list, from daily records, important "trigger" activities and then gradually eliminate cigarettes associated with the least to the most important of these. Some techniques are obvious or primitive, but may be helpful to some patients. Some smokers, for example, keep cigarettes, ashtray, and matches each in different areas of the house, lock cigarettes up, or restrict all smoking to one uncomfortable place. Substituting other activities for smoking, such as using an object to keep the hands busy, chewing gum or toothpicks, exercising, deep breathing, singing or doing needlework has also been used. Self-help aversive methods can also be used, such as wearing a large rubber band on the wrist and snapping it smartly so that it hurts whenever the urge to smoke becomes strong.

Self-help Manuals—One recent book (O. F. and C. S. Pomerleau, *Break the Smoking Habit,* Champaign, Ill: Research Press Company, 1977), offers an eight-week method combining record keeping, gradual withdrawl from cigarettes, an optional monetary reward, and several behavior modification techniques, including aversive conditioning. Another book, (B. G. Danaher and E. Lichtenstein, *Become an Ex-Smoker*, Englewood Cliffs, N.J.: Prentice-Hall, 1978) advises against gradually cutting down and recommends a combination of muscular relaxation with several other aversive and nonaversive behavioral methods, stressing maintenance. Still another (W. S. Ross, *You Can Quit Smoking in 14 Days*, New York: Berkeley Medallion, 1976) emphasizes the positive aspects of stopping smoking as a learning experience, not as an exercise of "will power." Fifty self-help methods are listed and, in addition to record keeping during the fourteen days, a nonsmoking scorecard is offered for maintenance with positive rewards for continuing nonsmoking behavior.

"Cold Turkey"—Some medical consultants favor abrupt abstinence over any method of gradual reduction and claim that most patients who do remain abstinent are those who stopped abruptly. For some people the process of reduction and all the various aids may serve only to focus more attention on what they're missing.

Conclusion—Many different types of aids, remedies, and programs are available to help the smoker who wants to stop. For some patients the most elaborate program may be the most successful.

Obesity—The most promising method of controlling the excessive eating that leads to excessive weight is the modification of our behavior toward food. Many other methods have been tried with high failure rates.

*From *The Medical Letter*, Dec. 1, 1978. Used with permission.

PHASE VI

It is, at last, time to put to a test those ideas selected as the ones best able to satisfy your intentions. Planning for the most part is over; the "moment of truth" has arrived. You have established the foundation of taking an action that will improve your problem.

Weight Control—For the severely obese person who has repeatedly tried and failed to lose weight, a modified fast way may be worth considering. Be sure the program is one properly supervised by a physician who is experienced in that approach. Joining Weight Watchers or TOPS (Take Off Pounds Sensibly; often achieve results that match any available medical treatment for obesity.

Behavior modification focuses on the control of the environment or situation surrounding eating habits. Begin your program with a three-week "diagnostic period." During this time you must systematically observe, record, and analyze your eating patterns.

Step 1: Keep a daily food-intake record that includes the following information:

1. Circumstances surrounding every bit of food eaten. Each time you eat or drink something, write it down immediately; don't wait until evening and list it all at one time. (The memory is faulty but the body uses every bit of food eaten.)

2. List the time, place, persons present, degree of hunger, and associated activities such as television, music, and talking.

3. List your mood: anxious, bored, tired, depressed, angry, or happy.

4. List the calorie value of each food or drink ingested during the day.

Step 2: Analyze your eating style—how one eats can be as important as what one eats. Eating fast, for example, may lead to eating more. People who are normal weight tend to eat more slowly and to chew their food more thoroughly than overweight persons.

Step 3: Analyze what you say to yourself about eating. Your thoughts are important predictors of your behavior. Two parts of your thoughts are vital in controlling eating behavior; your thoughts on personal goals and your private monologues.

Setting personal goals is of prime importance in developing a weight control program. It is most important that these goals be reasonable; not rigid or perfectionistic. To include goals that have "never" or "always" statements is to invite defeat if one small slip is made. Another aspect of goals is that they should be very specific. They should indicate precisely what is to be done. For example, a good goal is "I will eat dessert three times a week." That goal is preferable to "I will never eat dessert" (perfectionist) or "I will cut down on my desserts" (not specific).

The best goals are those that are relative. In other words, the goal should be in contrast to your past behavior. If you snack about four times a day, a reasonable goal is to cut that to two times a day. A goal of two snacks a day would be less reasonable if you were now snacking eight times a day.

Private monologues are another aspect of thought that can be self-defeating. Self-statements such as "Nothing works for me; I am a failure," or "I will always be a fat slob" are never going to help anyone. These lead to bad feelings about yourself and will defeat your change in behavior plans. In general, positive statements such as "I know I can do it; I have accomplished tougher things before," or "I am really doing better; I am so proud that I didn't eat my dessert." You will likely find it difficult to refuse food offered by friends and family. Taking food offered by others is one of the most common causes of overweight. You need the assistance of your family, close friends, and co-workers. You can request their help by explaining your method to them; especially those likely to offer you food. Ask them not to tease or closely observe you about food. Acknowledge their help by encouraging their positive efforts. Ask them not to criticize your mistakes or emphasize weight loss, but to focus on your change in behavior.

PHASE VII
Evaluation

Evaluations are not necessarily conclusions of a process; they may be the beginnings of another process. They end one journey and begin another; they are a link between journeys.

MEASURING PROGRESS

1. Statement of Goal—A statement of a goal is a declaration that you intend to attain a result or outcome. It tells you where you want to end up; not how to get there. You may want to

reach your goal tomorrow, next month, five years from now, etc. Goals are reached in stages, bit by bit, piece by piece.

2. Describe Your Objectives—Objectives need to be measurable; specific and clear. You can think of objectives as the work necessary or important in reaching the goal. In creating a new life-style, each person's requirements would differ from all others and standards for achievement would come from individual values, experiences, and expectations.

3. Achievement—Ask yourself: how far did I go? List the number of objectives reached. Ask yourself; how well did I do? List the benefits of your efforts; the knowledge acquired; the skills developed; the attitudes altered or reinforced.

4. Comparison of Goals with Achievement—Compare each point of your goals with your achievement. Review and reinforce your attitudes toward behavior change.

5. Future Plans—Objectives outline the paths to your goals; clean and measurable objectives are necessities. Clear foresight is not always possible. Do not become anxious over your results to this point. Simply review where you intend to ultimately end up with your behavior or life-style. Review your accomplishments; assess that work which seems to still remain and reaffirm your committment to the stated goal.

HEALTH'S HIGHEST PLANE

It seems pointless to change a behavior pattern, a bad habit, or a life-style without seeking the highest plane of health as a replacement of that former behavior. The highest plane, total wholeness brings it to a closer relationship with God; thus enabling us to attain a higher level of physical and mental health.

The apostle Paul, in Romans 6:12, stresses the vulnerability of our bodies. This vulnerability includes those desires we have for alcohol, food, or cigarettes. He did not see the body as being evil; he did view sin as finding a base of operation in the physical body. In his book, *Whatever Became of Sin?* Dr. Karl Menninger comments on the tendency to consider heroin and marijuana as "America's number one problem," ignoring alcohol and nicotine, which do far more harm to far more people. Dr. Menninger further comments about the sin of gluttony, one of the original "seven deadly sins." He considered gluttony as sinful in that it represents a degree of self-love which is self-destructive.

Paul talked of the "passions" which threaten our bodily health and existence. These are not to be understood only as sensual, for the word is also translated as "desire." The word may be used in a good as well as in a bad sense. Desire as such is not evil, but it may be turned to good or evil. The appetites and drives within us are not evil in themselves; they belong to us as the creation of God. Our bodies are not evil, nor are their impulses. The way we use our appetites, drives, and impulses is what makes the difference between good and evil. Paul stated further that he did not believe that we were determined genetically, socially, by Satan, by divine election, or by any other way to behave in a particular fashion. He placed the responsibility of our actions squarely on each of us. He assumed that a person does have a say about the quality of life he lives. We are free to make a choice between masters but we cannot choose to be free of a master. The life we live shows who or what is our master. Romans 6:16 is Paul's key statement. From it two principles emerge. The first is that we are slaves of whatever power we choose to serve and obey; the second is that there are only two alternatives available to us: servitude to sin, which "leads to death," or servitude to Christ, which "leads to righteousness." We have to choose between the two masters.

None of this is meaningful, however, unless we believe in the God revealed in Jesus Christ, the God of creation, who is of one mind about the proper fulfillment of mankind. We are responsible for our behavior; this brings hope not despair. The forces of change are not beyond our reach. What we cannot do alone, Christ is able to do. Bondage to a habit, a type of behavior, or a life-style is real but liberation is at hand in the person of Christ.

Jesus condensed the laws governing man's behavior and his relationship to God and man into two commandments as he answered the question of the scribe (Mark 12:28-31), "Of all the commandments, which is the most important?" and Jesus answered him, "The first of all the commandments is, Hear, O Israel; The Lord our

God is one Lord: And Thou shalt love the Lord thy God with all thy heart, and with all thy soul, and with all thy mind, and with all thy strength: this is the first commandment And the second is like, namely this, Thou shalt love thy neighbor as thyself. There is none other commandment greater than these."

Our love for Jesus must be exclusive. He is the Son of one and only God. He is God. He has made us and as his image-bearers on earth has given us the capacity and the commandment to love each other. Our conflicts with one another would vanish if we always treated each other as neighbors. This seems a practical way to live. God through Jesus doesn't force us to love him, nor are we forced to love our neighbors. We are free to love or not to love—it is not a duty. As we choose to love God and to love our neighbors we evoke the power of God in our lives. We have a new relationship to God and in this relationship our uncontrolled conflicts, temptations, and desires come under control.

Jesus promised not to leave his followers orphaned in the world (John 14:18). His promise was fulfilled on the day of Pentecost. His Spirit indwelt and empowered the first Christians on that great day, as he has all other believers since. Through his Spirit, God shapes and directs a believer's life. The Spirit inspires a mind-set toward God and the things of God. The chief role of the Spirit in a believer's life is that he is our helper. Inside the heart of every believer, a conflict of human nature goes on daily. The Spirit helps resolve the conflict in showing us how to live.

Paul, in Romans 8:5-7 (see NIV), tells us that there are only two possibilities in the spiritual realms of life; a "fleshly" mind-set and a spiritual mind-set. The mind-set of the flesh has "death" as its final destination (v. 6). It is "hostile to God" (v. 7) and it does not and cannot "please God" (v. 8).

Paul futher states that only those who possess God's Spirit are Christians (Rom. 8:9). Here he added the fact that any who continue to live according to human nature will surely die. He makes clear, however, that although believers are subject to temptations to "live according to the flesh," we can, with the Spirit's help, "put to death the deeds of the body" (v. 13, RSV). At least when we sin we can now repent, confess, and receive forgiveness (1 John 1:9). The Spirit is then free to enable us to put to death any practices that stand in the way of full life in the Spirit.

THE SPIRIT—OUR HELPER IN TIMES OF NEED

Paul refers to the Spirit's helping us because we "do not know how to pray as we ought" (Rom. 8:26, RSV). The word for "help" is instructive. It means "to take hold with," and the mental picture it evokes is that of a person with a burden or a load too heavy to carry by himself. So another takes hold of it (alongside of him) to help life or carry the load. Whatever our "weakness" or "infirmities," the Spirit goes alongside and helps with our burdens.

To illustrate, Paul used the example of prayer. Our burdens, at times, may seem too heavy to lift up to God "as we ought." Try as we may, the needs of our burdened hearts cannot be put into proper from. So what happens? The Spirit, like an unseen friend, takes hold of the burden and lifts it to God as prayer.

The Spirit moves us to pray, even though in certain situations we do not know what to pray for. In such times of confession, the Spirit again is our helper in lifting our conscious and unconscious prayers to heaven.

As believers we have two divine intercessors! Our Lord makes intercession for us in heaven (Heb. 7:25) while the Holy Spirit is the intercessor in our hearts. Always we have the Spirit within and alongside us, interceding for us "according to the will of God" (v. 27). This gives us the power to rise to the highest levels of faith and prayer. It is at this point that we reach the goal of total wholeness—our highest plane of health.

12
Faith—Its Role in Sickness

God is the creator of the universe and his adversary, the devil, is certainly at work. The "miracles" we witness today such as antibiotics, anesthesia, transplant surgery are of God, and certainly do alleviate suffering and prolong life.

I do not believe that the combination of God, Holy Spirit, and science are "false theories." Further, there is a great movement in medicine today realizing the importance of the spiritual well-being of a patient as far as getting over any pathological health state.

I speak to be counted as one who believes in the definite association of God and modern medicine.—CPN—*Surgeon*

As a physician, who also happens to profess his faith in Jesus Christ as his Lord and Savior, I do feel that the ultimate is to seek the will of God—and to do it! I believe *all* healing is from God; and there is no dichotomy into secular and sacred. (Matt. 9:1-8 Spiritual as well as ..).—WHD—*Pediatrician*

No feeling in the practice of medicine is deeper to me than the reality that God has a wonderful and marvelous part in the healing of every patient that I tend. In spite of always attempting to treat and prescribe according to the best available medical knowledge, there are times when the presence of God is so real that I almost think it would not even matter what type of drug was used since his presence and healing would be with that patient anyway.—CT—*Internist*

Medical literature is rampant with information about spontaneous regression of cancer, the dramatic effect of placebos, and even now, the effect in which the body produces a compound not unlike morphine to relieve pain. Anyone who has been in the practice of medicine for many years realizes that if a person refuses to die, he is likely to survive against all odds and perhaps even recover. On the other hand, someone who has given up any hope of survival is apt to die even though the disease which he has may be minor. It would appear that God has placed within our body the ability to heal itself, and that these abilities can be triggered by a proper suggestion or even perhaps by prayer.

I am aware of numerous incidences in my own practice where patients who had diseases that are of a chronic and permanent nature have become well after prayer. I am also aware of equally numerous incidences in which prayer was used by the patient or by a minister (and even by myself) in which no discernible benefit occurred. Nevertheless, I must say that it appears that prayer is equally effective, if not more effective, than usual medical treatment for some of these diseases. Certainly prayer appears to potentiate the effect of the medications that are being administered.

Incidently, although I am a Christian and for me this is the right and proper way to go, I have found that my prayers are more effective in those who are agnostic or even atheist.—GPT—*Ophthalmology*

In caring for podiatric patients far better results are attained when they understand that the doctor allows the Holy Spirit to work through him as he copes with their needs. Even the non-Christian patient is reassured by this commitment.

Response to therapy whatever it might be—from excising an ingrown nail bo a bunionectomy—is often directly related to the spiritual strength the podiatrist can convey to his patient. A Christian love and concern for that patient can still anxiety more than drugs.—CTC—*Podiatrist*

Since we know that man is a very complex creation made up of a body, mind, and spirit, any situation or set of circumstances which affect one area will, of necessity, spill over into the other two areas. The kind and understanding secularly oriented physician had been able in the past to deal with the needs of the body and mind but quite often, lacking a spiritual dimension of any degree himself, he has neglected to take care of this third and also very important part. In many cases the power of positive thinking and other types of confrontation therapy only serve as bandages rather than a definitive treatment. A physician who is spiritually tuned to God and is sensitive to God's leading is in a unique position in being able to minister to the needs of the body, mind, and the spirit. His degree of involvement in this particular area is limited only by his spiritual boldness and degree of spiritual maturity. In my own approach to the needs of my patients, I quite often give Christian counseling consisting of the pointing out of appropriate Scripture as well as dealing with them as to their personal relationship with God. I have seen a number of people who do not know Jesus Christ personally, commit their lives to Christ, either in the office or on follow-up counseling. In several cases I have seen lives transformed dramatically as a result of this ability to cut across all areas of need and believe this to be a most gratifying part of my practice of medicine.—LGB—*Dermatologist*

In any patient that comes to us we must learn to "sit where they sit." (This is what Ezekiel did when he was sent to the Israelites, Ezek. 3:15.) As we try to sit where our patients sit we can try to evaluate how they are perceiving their physical abnormalities and also come to know their emotional and spiritual needs as well. These latter two needs may far overweigh or even cause the physical illness. Physicians who have a relationship with Christ have the opportunity to share with these patients that show emotional and spiritual needs their outlook on life and hope that they find in Jesus Christ. When this opportunity arises, it should be done compassionately realizing that it is God who draws all people to himself.—HRL—*Gastroenterologist*

From the preventive medicine orientation of the pediatrician, I would like to speak to the spiritual need that is present in health as well as in disease. In my opinion, a holistic view of health focuses on the unity and harmony of the physical, mental, and spiritual components of one's being. Successful unity of these elements requires a more profound acceptance of the body with all its frailities and limitations than is comfortable for many persons in contemporary America. Many people can more readily understand the bodily manifestations of emotional stresses than can understand the therapeutic contribution that bodily exercise can make to emotional disturbance or spiritual unrest. The spiritual benefit of long distance running is just one example that is currently receiving publicity. The therapeutic effect of the arts of bodily self-expression is yet another example. One very important task of preventive pediatrics is to plant in childhood the seeds of acceptance of one's own body, in health, and most certainly in illness.

During sickness, the harmony of body, mind, and spirit receives one of its most severe challenges. Without question, the sick person needs the very finest of technical expertise to the neglect of personal concern and understanding is often insufficient. The patient must feel accepted by the physician and hopefully by the entire hospital staff, which in turn fosters the patient's self-acceptance. Though it is impossible for the physician to do so completely, the patient wants to sense that, "My doctor understands how I feel and what this disease is meaning to my life." (The meaning of an illness is very much a spiritual concern.) This response can occur only when the physician takes time to listen to the patient. There is no shortcut here. I believe without reservation that this is as much a part of the physician's therapeutic effort as any medicine and may be the most important aspect in many cases. For the pediatrician there is the additional challenge of helping the family of the young patient in their response to their child's illness. To me, one of the highest satisfactions within medicine comes from the realization that through the concerned practice of pediatrics, I may contribute to the physical, emotional, and spiritual harmony of my patient and his family during illness, or even more importantly, in preparation for the peaceful acceptance of death.—MRL—*Pediatrician*

I certainly do agree with you that a spiritual need is indeed present, especially taking care of cancer patients, patients who are terminally ill, I find this to be particularly true. Hope and encouragement do play a significant role in the care of many of these patients. I feel very often that the sickness may be allowed by God to open a person's eyes to life's most vital issues, especially for a man to be reconciled to God through his Son, Jesus Christ, and nothing short of this reconciliation is going to help the patient. I have also found that the patient who is a Christian has a decidedly better outlook, especially one who is paying the price and who has "set [his] affection on things above, not on things on the earth." The old adage, "to cure sometimes, to relieve often, and to comfort always" has been particularly of importance in my practice. I do not believe that we as doctors achieve any cure but are just instruments and agents used by God in healing. But to relieve the pain of a patient who is suffering or perhaps to just comfort him goes a long way in the management of a patient. Unfortunately, not many doctors have their eyes open to this aspect of practice which I believe is the most important. A Christian patient is also aware that "abundant life" does not necessarily have to include good health but in spite of adverse physical circumstances, the patient can possess abundant life by faith in Jesus Christ.—CSAE—*Hematologist-Oncologist*

The explication of suffering in the world is at the core of the Christian message. As physicians we are called to relieve sickness and its suffering. When our treatment is no longer efficacious, we are equally called to witness to the meaning of sickness in the lives of our patients.

The answer can be found in our call as Christians to give thanks and praise to God in all things—our trials as well as our joys. Although the origin of suffering lies in the sinfulness of man, God, in his infinite wisdom and mercy, can use suffering to instruct, perfect, and redeem us. We are all in need of pruning before we can bear good fruit.

Who among us can say he doesn't merit such suffering when our Lord, blameless as he was, willingly suffered his entire life for us? How often does the suffering of ill health make us appreciate the vanity of attachment to worldly things, and help us turn to the only true source of peace and joy? And, finally, isn't sickness often the cross we are to bear patiently and humbly as an act of reparation and an opportunity to give glory to God?—DM—*Internist*

My personal belief is that God is with us in whatever state we are in and will never forsake us if we trust him. The physician who is a Christian and who applies his own trust in God daily, praying for every patient and asking God to guide him in making decisions about diagnosis, utilization of proper diagnostic procedures, and therapy plus the ability to convey to the patient confidence and hope is truly His servant. A keen mind, constant updating of knowledge and a kind and considerate manner are basic good qualities of a physician, but the additional need of depending on Christ as his personal Savior and the constant awareness of his love are vital for the physician's ability to serve his patients. So often I am impressed by the response from patients when I imply that after a complete evaluation of their problems we can pray that God will heal and guide everyone involved in their care. I do not mean that I openly approach everyone this way but I often ask God to lead me into the proper path—sometimes I feel inadequate in expressing such faith and simply pray in silence when I feel the patient would reject me or feel I was a fanatic. As time goes on I have been able to overcome this problem somewhat. Asking about the patient's belief as a part of the routine history in a matter-of-fact manner may lead into a deeper discussion. I occasionally discover a real Christian I had not thought was inclined this way.

Once the spiritual status of a patient is assessed, I can be forthright in the care of an acknowledged Christian or can simply pray the non-Christian will sense his need. For many Christians I have found that total commitment and dependency on Christ's love is sorely lacking. Even more sad to me is the spiritual status of my medical collegues, many of whom are officers in their churches and profess their faith in the existence of God but fail to let their ambitions, fee schedules, and social life reflect God's purpose in their lives.

My own status is always being assessed as I find myself the sinner seeking his will and striving to push back temptations. Even more sad to me is the lack of appreciation on the part of my collegues who are professed Christians but who refuse to let Christ spill over into their relationship with patients. Dr. Paul Tournier says that every problem or every sickness is a spiritual one.

I would therefore say that sick people do indeed have spiritual needs and the single most effective person in helping to discover them is the individual closest involved in their illness or problems of any sort.—JCB—*Cardiologist*

When I think about a Christian physician's approach to medicine, it occurs to me that there is some bad news and some good news.

The bad news is: "It is appointed unto men once to die, but after this the judgment" (Heb. 9:27). This is God's decree in righteous response to man's sin. The good news is that Christ has provided a means whereby we can be reconciled to God, our sins forgiven, and eternal life attained. Knowledge of this fact provides the Christian physician with wonderful instruments with which to care for his patients. He can give them hope of a wonderful life of peace that will last forever. The Lord promises guidance when we ask for it with a pure heart and here again the Christian physician has a great advantage, for medicine is very complicated and fraught with many pitfalls, and there is only One who knows the future and knows how perfectly to avoid these pitfalls. I take every opportunity that I can to encourage my patients to come to the Lord for his salvation and his new life and his direction.—CBCM—*Gastroenterologist*

Attitude, or the condition of the mind, plays a significant role not only in sickness but also in health. When I think negatively, not only does the environment look gloomy, but I feel lousy. When I am positive, things look bright, and I feel cheerful and good.

Psychosomatic ailments are will known. The body responds to the mind in a multiplicity of ways. Anger, frustrations, and resentments can produce gastrointestinal upsets, tension headaches, backaches, and many other such ailments. If such effects are the result of mental stimuli, why cannot healing result from the opposite of these types of attitudes, or to be more specific, love instead of anger, acceptance in place of frustration, honor rather than resentment? The answer is that it can. The problem lies in my own inability to generate these attitudes when I can not manipulate and control my environment to suit my selfish wishes.

The solution lies in the supernatural power of the Lord Jesus Christ to change my life, give me his spirit, and add a totally new dimension to my life. "When someone becomes a Christian he becomes a brand new person inside. He is not the same any more. A new life has begun!" (2 Cor. 5:17, TLB). This new life is begun by the Spirit of God who now lives within me. "When the Holy Spirit controls our lives he will produce this kind of fruit in us: love, joy, peace, patience, kindness, goodness, faithfulness, gentleness and self-control" (Gal. 5:22-23, TLB). I have experienced this to be true in my life and I operate my practice on this truth.

The spiritual dimension is essential to a healthy life and wholesome attitudes. However, it is not a *self*-generated spiritual life . . . not the "power of positive thinking," transcendental meditation, or the like, for this would soon exhaust my mental resources. Rather, it is a "transformation and renewing of the mind" through yielding to the lordship (mastery, control) of the living Christ Jesus. Those who have experienced the "new birth" know this to be true.

One more thought: God is not so much interested in our physical comfort as in our character. These bodies of ours are destined to die and decay, but in eternity, our spirit lives on. Hence, God is more interested in molding us (the *external* us) into his likeness, than in preserving these bodies, which will eventually return to dust. This molding process often involves periods of suffering. When this is understood in the light of eternity, even these periods can be times of joy in the midst of pain.—SHF—*Plastic Surgeon*

13
Thoughts on Doctoring

> Sooner or later—insensible, unconsciously—the iron yoke of conformity is upon our necks; and in our minds, as in our bodies, the force of habit becomes irresisible. From our teachers and associates, from our reading, frrom the social atmosphere about us, we catch the beliefs of the day, and they become ingrained—part of our nature. For most of us this happens in the haphazard process we call education, and it goes on just as long as we retain any mental receptivity. It was never better expressed than in the famous lines that occurred to Henry Sidgwick in his sleep:
>
> We think so because all other people think so;
> Or because—or because—after all, we do think so;
> Or because we were told so, and think we must think so;
> Or because we once thought so, and think we still think so;
> Or because, having thought so, we think we will think so.
>
> . . . Walter Bagehot tells us that the pain of a new idea is one of the greatest pains to human nature. "It is, as people say, so upsetting; it makes you think that, after all, your favourite notions may be wrong, your firmest beliefs ill-founded; it is certain that till now there was no place allotted in your mind to the new startling inhabitant; and now that it has conquered an entrance, youdo not at once see which of your old ideas it will not turn out, with which of them it can be reconciled, and with which it is at essential enmity."
>
> Osler
Harveian Oration, 1906.

During the past twenty years, much of my time has been spent diagnosing and treating sickness in a large number of patients. It has been a satisfactory work generally—but there is a bothersome feeling that many of my patients were not helped to be as well as they might be Perhaps the iron yoke of conformity mentioned above by Dr.

Osler stifled my imaginative powers. It is only recently that I have been able to isolate the deficiency in my treatments. In the first place, many people choose habits, eating patterns, and activity levels that, over the years, lead to chronic diseases which are irreversible. They could have chosen better had they known the danger of their life-style leading to disease or had their determination been stronger. Secondly, sickness touches all of us eventually, but healthy mental attitudes will assure healthy physical bodies and delay or prevent the onset of illness.

Many claim to be the best teachers of mental health, but my personal view is that the message of the Bible is the connecting link for better physical health because it develops mental health scripturally. Mastering poor health can be done prospectively, before it develops, by healthy habits and styles of life or after it develops by restoring healthy mental attitudes through Scripture.

CATEGORIES OF PATIENTS

It is not always easy to come to a final diagnosis of a patients's symptoms. Many of my patients had symptoms which varied from visit to visit, usually not indicating a serious medical disorder.

Many symptoms were healed through the body's curative power or disappeared with medications prescribed for relief of the discomfort. Many of these patients were helped by a reasonable explanation of their problem without a prescription for drugs. For some, their symptoms were thought to indicate a serious medical problem, and were then investigated with appropriate laboratory, X-ray, or other diagnostic studies. In most of these patients, no serious medical problem was uncovered. Many times I would be convinced that I was overlooking an important clue and the intensity of the pursuit of the problem would awaken me in the middle of the night. I would turn the problem over and over in my mind seeking for the missing piece of the puzzle.

In the care of certain patients, I had to maintain a high tolerance of uncertainty, for I would be sure of the presence of undiagnosed disease. But I would often reexamine the patient over the course of many months before the evidence was clear. One category of patients had diseases for which there was specific treatment and cure was expected. Another group was found to have degenerative diseases for which there was no specific therapy. Yet another group was found to have symptoms as a result of personality dysfunction, stemming from an unpleasant job situattion, an economic plight, a family atmosphere of fussing and tension, the use of alcohol, or a combination of a number of these. I found my choices of therapy to be unsettling; I had no confidence in the treatments. When I looked at what other doctors did for these problems arising from life's troubles, I wasn't impressed with their approaches or results. Many of my patients had such troubles and I seemed to have no adequate solution.

The explosion of research into disturbances of mood evolved in an effort to cope with the problem of personality dysfunction. An increasing number of drugs, names such as Aventyl, Elavil, Triavil, Mellaril, Equanil, and Valium became available. New names were added at regular intervals. Research in this area has suggested that a particular class of substances called the biogenic amines, are central to the regulation and maintenance of mood. The most important of these delicate compounds, serotonin and norepinephrine, are present at certain critical receptor sites in the brain, and are most highly concentrated in areas associated with such drives as hunger, thirst, and sex.

The evidence so far suggests that it is the balance between these compounds at the nerve-cell connections, which Harvard psychobiologist Gerald L. Klerman likens to a "particular carburetor mix" that is most important in maintaining a stable mood. Too much or too little of these compounds disturbs the balance and creates the conditions for acute despair or sets the stage for depression with its miserable, powerless feelings of inferiority. The "mental changes" of depression are accompanied by a profoundly altered physical state, for it is a toatal disorder involving almost every body system.

These drugs were not replacing the "talking" types of therapy; for they too seem to be growing in number and variety. Approximately two years ago, it was estimated that there were over two hundred different approaches in psychiatry and psychology. Many of these used drugs listed above in combination with counseling. Such a variety of therapy suggested a confused state of affairs in the counseling field. Many physicians in all fields questioned the effectiveness of this approach to the problem of disturbed mental health. I questioned the wisdom of using drugs to correct biochemical abnormalities caused by patients' life stresses. Anxieties and depressions, occurring as a result of feelings, thoughts, faulty perceptions, and faulty interpretation of life, could hardly be cured with a pill to quiet the worry. It seemed to me that the stress should be used as a lesson; strengthening the mind, providing an experience, and showing the way to avoid the same mistake the next time.

I sometimes referred patients with emotional problems for psychiatric evaluation and treatment. The psychiatrist, using standard counseling practices, must interpret the patients's problems and suggest solutions to those problems in the light of his own system of values. The psychiatrist's system of values could be totally dissimilar to that of the patient. If so, the diagnosis of the emotional problem, as well as the suggested therapy might be inappropriate.

Some medical problems are related to changing social and moral standards. Patients with symptoms arising from these causes, as well as those with little hope, should question their illness as a message that their basic need is an improved relationship with God. The traditional medical approach is not sufficient to satisty that need.

Many of those patients in the second category, those with specific diseases without specific therapy, were found to have "degenerative disorders"—coronary heart disease, arthritis, and emphysema. These are treated with modern medicines in an attempt to control the disease, though cure is not possible and improvement is not always possible. Degenerative disorders are often complicated by excessive weight, cigarette smoking, alcohol, or too little exercise. Treatment, to be successful, must control these complicating factors. Patients' habits must change; their life-style must be made healthier. Habits are undoubtedly hard to change. Very few of my patients seemed to be willing to make an investment in their health, even though they could expect to gradually become disabled or to live a life made miserable by poor health. The failure to change patients' minds, the failure to persuade them, was discouraging, but I knew that a great part of the responsibility for change belongs to the patient. Perhaps my concept of the role of the doctor was faulty. The practice of medicine is an interesting, stimulating profession, but I had no wish to indulge in an intellectual exercise without benefiting the patient. Perhaps I was overlooking an important factor without knowing it.

Dr. Lawrence Henderson, famous biochemist, stressed the need for doctors to become more aware of the effect of family relationships, crowded living conditions, and other sociologic problems on their patients' illnesses. It is evident that he regarded the medical situation as something of a gamble; he stated, "Somewhere between 1910 and 1912 in this country . . . random patient with a random disease, consulting a doctor chosen at random, had for the first time in the history of mankind, a better than fifty-fifty chance of profiting from the encounter." Dr. Henderson implied that progress had been made in medical diagnosis and treatment since 1912. It is true that many technologic advances have been made, but it is discouraging to find that statistics have not proved that the consultations or encounters between doctors and patients have appreciably changed the course of life and death. Now it would be absurd to suggest to any practicing physician that his presence and therapy have never made the difference between life and death for any of his patients. The fact remains, however, sickness is still widespread and is often a threat to life.

Dr. F. J. Ingelfinger suggested in the *New England Journal of Medicine,* of February 24, 1977, that 80 percent of all patients have either self-limited disorders or conditions not improvable, even by modern medicine. The physician's actions, unless harmful, will therefore not affect the basic course of such conditions. In slightly over 10 percent of the cases, however, medical intervention is dramatically successful whether the surgeon removes stones or repairs bones, or the internist uses antibiotics, misdiagnosed or inadequately treated by a doctor, or the patient may merely have misfortune. Whatever the reason, the patient ends up with problems related to the diagnosis or treatment.

The probability of problems causes me deep concern—people came expecting help—not additional trouble. Early in the establishment of medicine as a profession, the famous Greek physicians, as they made their visits to see patients in the surrounding islands, recognized their inability to cure many diseases. They established the attitude of caution, "do not harm," which is still used today in guiding the behavior of doctors. This principle was even translated in one instance to read, "to help or at least do no harm," as if expressing a relative inadequacy of medicine to reverse the evil of sickness. The modern doctor finds these words as useful today as did Hippocrates 2,400 years ago.

It is my hope, as I approach each patient's problems, that I will be able to prescribe a medicine, recommend an operation, or offer a suggestion that will ease his suffering, wipe away the threat to his life, and restore him to wholeness. It is not always to be so, but in any event, the way I approach his problem assures him of my concern and keeps alive his hope that he will be healed. Faith that healing will result is the outcome of many office visits.

A doctor's skills are exposed daily to unmistakable good and evil, good in the form of health and evil in the form of sickness. If, in spite of my efforts, evil triumphs and my patient dies, I don't shake my fist at God for having failed me and allowed death to come to my patient. I view death as inevitable but also as a threat which is to be conquered if at all possible. My skills are dedicated to that end. Here I return to my two themes. A person's own actions may cause disease, injury, or misfortune to affect his life; he may have ignored the laws of nature which God uses to guarantee order in the universe. In this event, or in any case of sickness, it is a decided comfort to me, and usually to the patient, that I can call upon the Creator for his comfort, wisdom and direction in combating the evil of disease inhabiting the patient's body. This spiritual help brings hope to the patient and opens the way to his awareness of his spiritual needs and to the role of faith in his sickness.

Inasmuch as medical skills affect areas of human good and evil, with the consequent suffering from such influences, there is a basis for considering the medical arts sacred in many traditions, for they are said to come directly from the hand of God and are intended to heal the creatures of God. The prayer of the Jewish physician, Moses Maimonides (1135-1204) ends, "Almighty God, Thou has chosen me in Thy mercy to watch over the life and death of Thy creatures. I now apply myself to my profession. Support me in this great task so that it may benefit mankind." A long tradition thus supports the view that physicians are not morally free to dispose of their skills entirely as they see fit, but are bound by the origin, nature, and purpose of their art to use them only for human benefit.

If, as Dr. Ingelfinger suggests, 80 percent of my patients have self-limiting problems, most of which are going to get better by themselves, or have a disorder which has no specific therapy, then much of my skill as a doctor may be to "watch over the life and death" of God's creatures just as Maimonides did. I must be technically skillful enough to diagnose the diseases afflicting the 10 percent for whom there is specific treatment and especially careful in my choice of tests and therapies in order to reduce the chance of reactions and complications to their lowest point.

Where do I get instruction in "watching over" or caring for those of my patients who will be benefited primarily by my encouragement, my instructions, and my confidence that I can do something for them? I must evaluate their doubts and fears as I would symptoms of any sort. If there is a spiritual void which needs to be filled with assurance of help for their problems, I feel the need to be able to point them in the direction of faith. They may fear that they have a fatal illness and that death is just around the corner, or that life will be a living death of pain, loss of job, inability to provide for their family, or a state of dependency on family members. Hopelessness must not become the basis of life—doubts and fears must be replaced by faith in God through Jesus Christ.

Degenerative illnesses may be responsible for years of modified existence—a reduction in physical activity, a changed way of eating, occasional hospital admissions, frequent visits to the doctor's office, or the taking of medicine daily. Chronic illness causes psychological changes which accompany physiological changes in the body, and, if not recognized, may produce symptoms which confuse the doctor and further depress the patient. If my actions and words indicate that I don't understand the psychological aspects of the illness, the result may be a negative mental state which diminishes or destroys the patient's faith that I will be able to help him or cure him. This faith of expectancy plays a part in all forms of healing, whether the healing agent is a medical doctor, a faith healer, the patient himself, or a religious shrine such as Lourdes, where thousands journey each year in the hope that a miracle will restore their sight or the use of a withered arm or leg.

Traditionally, medicine as we know it has been dominated by a viewpoint that dates back to the seventeenth-century French philosopher-scientist, René Descartes. Descartes preached a division between mind and matter, with the body being a form of matter. According to this view, the doctor is essentially a mechanic who patches up the body after it has been damaged by illness and injury. We can readily see the limitations of this view if only 10 percent of patients are truly recipients of the impressive triumphs of modern medicine. This is a failure to consider the individaul as a psychobiologic being—with thoughts, perceptions, and feelings intimately connected with his biochemistry and physiology. This concept of the person as a psychobiological system is at the heart of the movemnt which has been termed "Holistic Medicine." This movement has gained momentum due to disenchantment which the approach to medicine recognizes that an illness or injury that wounds the body may also scar the mind and that a patient's mental state may determine how quickly—or how slowly—he recovers from an illness.

According to holistic theory, a healthy person is one whose total system—both mind and body—is in a state of dynamic equilibrium. In this state, the healing strength and functions of the body are superior to the destructive forces. During an illness, the person's total system is upset, and, at least temporarily, the destructive forces have the upper hand. Healing, then, is the restoring of the dynamic equilibrium; it may occur spontaneously or with the aid of a medical or nonmedical healer. Much of the disillusion prompting the holistic movement stemmed from the tendency of American doctors to become captivated by modern medical technology, overlooking the fact that, in the final analysis, the success of a cure depended on the healing power within the patient. Credit for healing or cure, however, centuries ago was ascribed to God, as Ambroise Pareé, the great sixteenth-century French surgeon noted in closing his case reports, "I dressed the wound and God healed it."

Medicine, I am sad to admit, has lost it grasp on reality. Life is held sacred at any cost, in any form. We spend millions of dollars each year keeping alive patients whose brains have ceased to function. Thousands of people with incurable cancers are treated with chemotherapy, irradiation, and radical surgery, yielding a few additional months of life of poor quality, at an expense that is hardly justified.

Physicians see these problems daily and are repulsed by the futility, yet only rarely do we reflect on this futility sufficient to change our approach to the problem.

Twisted reality encourages an aggressive approach to the care of patients with such shocking medical problems as the demented elderly woman, unable to let her wishes be known, who was sent into the hospital from a nursing home because a bed sore had eroded through the skin, exposing the bone underneath. She died two months and $40,000 later after the abscesses had extended through the hip to the groin and had finally, mercifully, killed her.

It is crucial that people understand the realities of today's medicine. The cost of health care continues to go up, due in part to misapplication of advanced technology to patients who are beyond its reach. The doctor, instead of allowing himself to be carried along with the tide of medical practice, should evaluate his role in the light of the Bible's message about life and death. It is not necessary that he play God in the care of his patients.

I believe that those patients with a close relationship to God will face the consequences of a serious medical problem with greater courage, less fear, and greater equanimity than patients without this faith. God, the Creator, is still in charge of healing.

Dealing with the evils of sorrow, suffering, loneliness, despair, and death produces an emotional strain in the doctor's life which may not be measurable with every case but is of compounded seriousness over the years. He is in danger of becoming less sensitive, looking at his work as a treadmill instead of a calling. The grind can kill the thrill, and the routine may well harden the attitude of a doctor toward not only his patients but the miracles of healing and life. The doctor's faith in God helps maintain his perspective of his job as a calling, working as Maimonides said, "on God's creatues."

Even with this, there are times in a doctor's work when death comes to a young person or healing fails to come as expected and we question: Where is God? Why is he avoiding us? Why won't he answer? The answer we get may be dead silence. We seek the answers from the Bible and find that while Paul was used to healing people, his request for healing was denied; and death was not always overcome in the Bible; John the Baptist was executed.

Two passages from the Bible are surprising in their perspective on this issue: the burial of Lazarus (John 11) and the roadside talk about Jesus; death on the way to Emmaus (Luke 24:13-15). Both stories have dramatic and happy endings. But we can learn from the waiting period in each story, the four days when Lazarus's body rotted in the grave and his family cried tears of disappointment over Jesus' seeming callousness, and the days when the disciples were convinced the entire kingdom had collapsed. These four days parallel the times of anxious waiting we spend facing pain or suffering.

To view the role of pain and suffering properly, we must await the whole story. Promises of it abound in the Bible: "The God of all grace, who called you to his eternal glory in Christ, after you have suffered a little while, will himself restore you and make you strong, firm and steadfast" (1 Pet. 5:10, NIV). "These troubles and sufferings of ours are, after all, quite small and won't last very long. Yet this short time of distress will result in God's richest blessings upon us forever and ever! So we do look not at what we can see right now, the troubles all around us, but we look forward to the joys in heaven which we have not yet seen. The troubles will soon be over, but the joys to come will last forever" (2 Cor. 4:17,18, TLB).

Peter, Paul, and millions of others have been so confident of the end result that they staked their health, their fortunes, their very lives on Christ's promises. As Paul said, "In my opinion whatever we may have to go through now is less than nothing compared with the magnificent future God has planned for us. The whole creation is on tiptoe to see the wonderful sight of the sons of God coming into their own" (Rom. 8:18,19, Phillips). It may be that there is a message in our illness or pain, asking us to let it turn us to Christ. It is my faith in God through Christ that convinces me that my job as a doctor is to help my patients understand the message of their sickness as well as to seek a cure or relief of their suffering.

Supplementary Reading

Chapter 1   Persons in God's World
The Wisdom of the Body, Walter Cannon; W. W. Norton and Company, 1939.
Man, Medicine and Environment, Rene Dubos; Prager Publishers, 1978.
Man Adapting, Rene Dubos; Yale University Press, 1965.

Chapter 2   The Diseased Heart
Live Longer, Now, Jon N. Leonard, Jack L. Hofer, and Nathan Pritiken; Grosset and Dunlap, New York, 1974.

Chapter 3   Human Nature—Worried Sick
Aristotle for Everybody, Mortimer J. Adler; Macmillan, 1978.
The Broken Heart, James J. Lynch; Basic Books, 1977.
Understandings of Man, Perry Le Fevre; The Westminster Press.
Psychology of Consciousness, Robert E. Ornstein; Harcourt Brace Jovanovic, Inc., 1977.
The Identity of Man, J. Bronowski; The Natural History Press.
The Meaning of Persons, Paul Tournier; Harper and Row, 1957.

Chapter 4   Cancer— A Threat to Life
Cancer Rates and Risks, DHEW Publication Number 75-691, NIH: 2nd Edition, 1974.
Proceedings of the American Cancer Society's National Conference on Human Values and Cancer, 1972.
Persons at High Risk of Cancer, Fraumeni; Academic Press, 1975.

Chapter 5   Human Nature—Seeking Healing
The Psychological Society, Martin L. Gross, Random House.
The Nature and Destiny of Man, Reinhold Niebuhr; Scribners, 1969.
The Voice of Illness, Siirale Aarne; Fortress Press, 1964.

Chapter 7 A Healthier Heart
Endurance Fitness, Roy I. Shephard; University of Toronto Press, 1969.
Interval Training, Edward L. Fox and Donald K. Matthews; W. B. Saunders Company, 1976.
Exercise Your Way to Fitness and Heart Health, Lenore R. Zohman; American Heart Association, 1974.
Exercise Testing and Training of Apparently Healthy Individuals: A Handbook for Physicians; American Heart Association, 1972.

Chapter 8 Eating to Live
Feel Younger, Live Longer, Jack Tresider, Editor; Rand McNally, 1976.
The High Energy Diet for Dynamic Living, Max M. Novich, Ted Kaufman; Grosset and Dunlap, 1976.
Compositions of Foods, Agricultural Handbook, Number 8; United States Department of Agriculture.

Chapter 9 God's Nature—Healing
Healing and Christianity: In Ancient Thought and in Modern Times, Morton T. Kelsey; Harper and Row, 1976.
The Power to Heal, Francis MacNutt, O.P; Ava Maria Press, 1977.
In Two Minds, Os Guinness; Inter Varsity Press, 1976.
The Will of God, Leslie D. Weaterhead; Abingdon Press, 1944.
Where Is God When It Hurts? Philip Yancey, Zondervan, 1977.
Spiritual Counterfeits Project Journal, August, 1978.

Chapter 10 The Doctor—God's Instrument
Doing Better and Feeling Worse, Health in the United States, Edited by John H. Knowles, M.D.; W. W. Norton and Co., Inc., 1977.
What Medicine Is All About, Mark D. Altschule, M.D.; The Francis A. Countway Library of Medicine, 1975.
The Horizons of Health, Edited by Henry Weeksler, Joel Gurin, George F. Cahil, Jr.; Harvard University Press, 1977.
The Christian as a Doctor, James T. Stephens and Edward Leroy Long, Jr.; Haddam House Book, 1960.

Chapter 11 A Blueprint for Change
The Universal Traveler, Don Soberg and Jim Bagnall; William Kaufman, Inc., 1976.

SUPPLEMENTARY READING

The Medical Letter, Vol. 20, No. 24 (Issue 519); December 1, 1978.

Whatever Became of Sin? Karl Menninger; Hawthorne Books, Inc., 1973.

Permanent Weight Control, Michael J. Mahoney and Kathryn Mahoney; W. W. Norton and Company.

FIRST BAPTIST CHURCH LIBRARY
TOMBALL, TEXAS